P-B-A-R
REVISITED

YOUR THOUGHTS DETERMINE YOUR FUTURE!

Robert Henry, MD, FACPE

Trafford
PUBLISHING

 www.trafford.com

North America & international
toll-free: 1 888 232 4444 (USA & Canada)
phone: 250 383 6864 ♦ fax: 250 383 6804 ♦ email: info@trafford.com

The United Kingdom & Europe
phone: +44 (0)1865 722 113 ♦ local rate: 0845 230 9601
facsimile: +44 (0)1865 722 868 ♦ email: info.uk@trafford.com

10 9 8 7 6 5

ACKNOWLEDGEMENTS

I have lived nearly 83 years, blessed and supported by a myriad wonderful human beings who were all my mentors at one time or another. To acknowledge each one separately would take another volume and individual praise would be relatively useless for the purposes of showing my gratitude for their many inputs. It has been said that *"no man is an island"*, that we are all connected with one another, and that is so true, because life is too complex to be handled without a strong group of contributors to help erect your own scaffolding on which to live.

There is one person in my life that stands above all the rest and that is my wife, Lou Cator-Henry who has been my champion and constant source of direction. She and I have used P-B-A-R concept across the country with hospitals, schools and corporate entities for, perhaps 15 years with great results. It was designed to present a methodology by which we could see how our lives from birth to the present were shaped primarily by parents, family and society's demands for conformity and shed light on the role that our early life programming instilled false information, distortions of how to raise kids and because we learn what is given to us, those same flaws of our programming become part of our belief system for the rest of our lives leaving us with incomplete competence for making our lives what they have the potential to be.

I thank you reader, for having interest in improving the way we prepare children for the tasks at hand. We need an overhaul of the system that locks the majority of people in the prisons of their own mind. Won't you consider lending your own ideas and support to changing the quality of life that can come with new perspectives?

INDEX

Chapter 1   The Current Scene 1

Chapter 2   Where is it Heading 6

Chapter 3   How Did It All Happen?. 15

Chapter 4   What is P-BAR?. 24

Chapter 5   Programming. 26

Chapter 6   Reflections on Your "Programming" 38

Chapter 7   Beliefs ("B"). 44

Chapter 8   How You Got Your Beliefs 53

Chapter 9   Actions ("A") 57

Chapter 10   Results ("R") 60

Chapter 11   Halfway There!. 64

Chapter 12   Things I needed to learn 72

Chapter 13   Things We All Need to Know 81

Chapter 14   EGOs at Work 85

Chapter 15   Ego Defenses 93

Chapter 16   It's Not Hard to Understand 100

Chapter 17   Homes and the Raising of Children. 103

Chapter 18   What Needs to Be Done? 107

Chapter 19   Today's Scene .111

             Appendix 123

7

CHAPTER 1

THE CURRENT SCENE

This magnificent ball, planet Earth, on which we live, is a place of indescribable beauty. I so envy the astronauts that were able to observe it from space in all its pristine beauty; that blue sphere floating in the space of the Universe moving in its ever-predictable orbit among the other celestial bodies.

But those of us who are earth bound still can see its beauty up close and personal. All of the geological features of mountains, valleys, chasms, and streams are there for us to appreciate and draw sustenance from. The wonders of nature, the cycles of seasons, the self-restorative qualities that the earth has, all attest to the continuous presence of the Universal Mind, the Energy Source that activates all of us.

It was God's gift to all of us and, it was implied that we would have dominion over the Earth and the creatures therein. I stress "*dominion*" and, not "*domination*" as we seem to have interpreted it. Inherent in that mandate is the notion that the gift was of inestimable value and it should be cared for to preserve its treasures for all time and posterity.

The miracles of the systems that are operative in the world are incredible. The gravity that holds us in place, the nurturance of the planet for food provision and abundance, the water cycle where water evaporates and re-condenses as rain and snow to maintain the hydration of the earth, the physical, chemical, and energy-related systems that power all of life—all of these miracles are given freely by the Creator and designed to perpetuate our human existence on this planetary space ship.

The Earth has gone through millions of years of transition and adaptation in the evolutionary process according to the grand plan of the Creator.

All is provided for and there is abundance for us to enjoy and bask in.

But, you may have noticed that there is another process going on simultaneously. Forces that threaten the integrity of the world and are effecting degradation of the most important elements of the planet are also impinging the very processes that define our world.

Our failure at providing dominion and safety for our environment is the basis of the deterioration of the quality of life and, further threatens the intactness of our planet. Pollution of our air, seas and landmasses, mismanagement of the natural resources, careless interruption of the normal cycles of regeneration, and our greed and avarice continually contribute to the demise of our "space home".

Furthermore, it is not only the natural aspects of the earth that are suffering under our neglect but, perhaps even more importantly, we are escalating the deterioration of relationships between ourselves and all other inhabitants of the planet earth.

A global view of Earth would show us a sight not unlike a gigantic anthill with six billion people swarming in and out of their locations, following their habitual pathways in search of sustenance, and meaning, some of which leads nowhere except in frantic circles. In the daily movements, these human creatures are colliding, intersecting one another's scrambling, some actually enjoying the encounters but, for the most part the majority trying to deal with, cope with, and even eliminate others who are deemed toxic and deadly.

Everywhere you turn your attention today there are wars, mini-conflicts, incredible displays of humans destroying humans. It happens in places where there have been on- going cultural, political, racial, ethnic and economic struggles for centuries. It fosters conflagrations about land, territories, resources, still struggling to bring closure to ancient jealousies, and religious challenges.

None of this is new to the world. History is replete with tales of destructive influences tearing each other apart, sacrificing millions of lives in the process and yet never learning how to live in harmony and peace with one another. There are also those periodic examples of genocide that defy understanding such as the Holocaust in Germany and the recent killing of more than 800,00 people in Rwanda by their own kind.

It has been suggested that there have been a number of times in the life of the planet when there have been catastrophic events of such magnitude that all life at that time came to an end. It is no stretch of imagination to think it could happen again.

When the people of this world are so engaged in the devastation of person-to- person, country-to-county, nation-to-nation, race-to-race, ethnic-group to other group interactions, it is difficult to think harmony, peace, love and collaboration can emerge. The conditions are ripe for a calamitous disaster to take place. No amount of reasonable persuasion or negotiation is being effectively used at this time to alter the worldwide destructive patterns. Now that many countries have acquired weapons of mass destruction, it is plausible that life, as we know it could be eradicated by the worldwide spread of mayhem.

One can ask the questions about how it all came about? Why, when we have all the necessary ingredients for cooperative and loving living, are we so locked into mutual annihilations? Where does all of the negative, destructive power come from? What reasons are there for the ubiquitous desire to eliminate one another? We can cite the greed, anger, jealousies, envy, the seeking of power over others, the belief in long-deserved retribution to others for real or imagined injuries, the desire for settling old quarrels by genocide; there is no lack of reasons to justify employing evil actions against one another. A major broadly-held belief is that it is acceptable and warranted to kill and plunder when "necessary" to settle these old accounts by eliminating the "offending" parties.

Such would never have been the intent of a Creator of the Universe. Although understanding the intention of God is beyond our capabilities, common sense tells us that such a Creator would not design such a magnificent system and then also design into it the behavior of human entities that will dismantle it over time.

Some continue to ask the question, "Why doesn't God make us stop all of what we are doing and make us get along with each other?"

The answer to that question is something that we have puzzled over for centuries. It seems that if God took that action to settle our disputes and our self-destruction, he would be going against one of his gifts and promises to us, namely the "free will" that he has given us. To intercede in our craziness would be to overrule our "free will" to do as we wish. God is not an "Indian-giver". What then can possibly bring about the salvation of the world, saving it from our own annihilating actions? It would require a critical mass of existing persons to unite in unfailing love and to replace the hate, anger, greed, and envy and for them to extend their own love to all others until love and understanding pervade human thinking.

Perhaps it would help if we consider the fact that in the history of the planet, there have been many incidences in which the established cultures and civilizations have gone through their own ups and downs and finally hit rock bottom as their way of life perished. If you look at the patterns over the centuries it appears that each one of these ancient lifetimes on this planet had similarities. Each started with a simple alteration in the way life was being lived at the time. As the "new way" gained in popularity and acquired adherents that promoted the culture, the arts, the language, laws and mores that were predominant in the advancing culture, the "new way's" influence spread. As more people joined in the movement, it gathered momentum and became powerful, even dominant in its time and enjoyed great glory and prosperity.

However, as history has so well documented, as each and every one of these civilizations expanded, there seemed to be some seed of inner destructive erosion that robbed it of its power, glory, and effectiveness and ultimately each culture collapsed under the weight of its own pathology. This becomes painfully apparent in looking back at the succession of powerful empires and cultures that rose into prominence and then, as described above, spiraled into oblivion for the very destructive reasons we are observing in our own times.

Does it have to happen in this repetitive way? I think the answer is "not necessarily" but it will require enormous changes that only we inhabitants can bring about by our waking to the threat and making the personal and collective changes in our ways of living. It isn't the earth and its environment that is causing the trouble.

It is "us" with our selfishness, our greed, our absorption with anger as an answer to settle issues and our willingness, if necessary, to escalate our sense of separation from one another into worldwide massacres for the sake of gaining control over others to avoid being controlled by them. We are six billion individuals trying to control or eliminate the presence of the others that we have identified as "enemies" when in fact, we are all alike, totally interrelated to the rest of mankind and potentially capable of learning to live together in harmony and in peace.

CHAPTER 2

WHERE IS IT HEADING

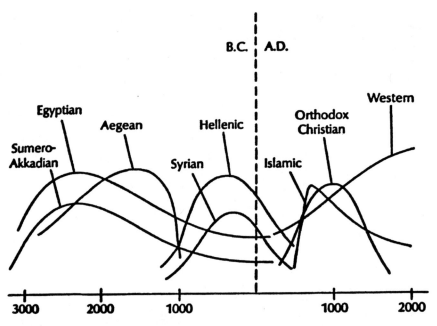

Rise-and-fall patterns of the major civilizations around the Mediterranean.

This graphic tells it all. This is a depiction of what is termed the Life Cycle Curve and it is applicable to almost everything in our lives.

This particular picture tells us that each of the major cultures, empires, and controlling dynasties of the past followed this Life Cycle Curve.

Each, in its turn had a modest onset in which the thinkers and doers of the time put forth their new ideas about how things ought to be. Over time their notions became accepted and expanded into the structure of their particular time span. Throughout history, each separate culture had a similar beginning, followed by a span of time in which it was creative, enlightened and dominant. And then through the same carelessness, greed, and destructive relationships with the rest of the world it cycled into the same downward plunge into oblivion.

In fact, this is the way that most entities begin whether we are talking about a religion, a nation's ascension to power, the discovery of concepts about sciences of all kinds, or the invention of manufactured products. It also applies to our very own life here on earth. We start in an infant state and, over time grow, assimilate the lore and rules of our time and eventually we, as adults reach the top of our development and begin a descent into later life and eventually to our demise.

Simply, it says that everything has a beginning characterized by struggle and challenge, followed by a variable period of time in which it flourishes and then seems to enter a phase of disintegration and death. I believe that we unconsciously realize the shape of the path for ourselves. It is inevitable that we individually grow, thrive and then experience the downward portion of our life cycle. Certainly in the case of our own lives we are well aware that there comes a time when we will be no more, ushered in by aging, losing energy, competence and stamina. We know this because it is an ever-present reality in the lives of all of us.

What we don't recognize as easily, is that everything else around us is participating in a similar pattern.

Pick a time when you think the Western World cycle as portrayed by our American Way began. It seems to have started with the challenges the Pilgrims encountered and the struggles that accompanied the plight of the early colonies. The separation from our English oppression via the Revolutionary War initiated the new curve for the American continent. Thereafter, the upward turn of the curve represented the growth and emergence of the culture during the 17th through the 20th centuries and gave rise to the way of life that we experience today.

You don't have to look too far to see evidence of the turmoil and struggle that is going on everyday in our world. There are multiple wars being waged, sometimes in countries that we didn't even know existed before now.

Closer at hand, we can get sharper views of the interactions between people at our job sites, our recreational venues, our neighborhoods and even in our churches. Over 50 % of the marriages of today are ending in divorce with the accompanying trauma for the people (parents and children) involved in those breakups. The discord is at all levels of our corporations from the boardrooms to the assembly floors. We are witnessing the degradation of the quality of our society—morally, health-wise, socially, economically, culturally, politically, and spiritually and, in terms of what America once stood for (as a beacon of progress and prosperity for the world), we now seem to be on course resembling what has happened to other cultures when they carelessly allowed their own attitudes to bury them.

Why? The **"why"** is difficult to answer although we <u>must work</u> together on the **"why"** if there to be any hope of changing the present course.

The **"how"** is easier because the myriad causes of the disintegration of our way of life all come about as a result of the kind of people we are becoming, what we are allowing to fall apart on our watch and the pernicious effect that our own anger, greed, selfishness, indifference, and neglect are fostering.

We're all aware of the impending situations and all are cognizant of what it means for the future of, not only our country, but for the entire human race, yet we seem to be oblivious to the fact that it is **<u>only people</u>** that are the purveyors of the decaying processes in our lives. It isn't the raccoons, the wolves, and the loons returning to their nesting areas. It isn't the migrating birds, the monarch butterflies, nor is it related to the climatic, volcanic or meteorological activity around the globe. It is not bad luck, bad karma or planetary curses. It is the people who populate the globe that are doing-the-doing and we are doing it to one another.

Now here is another concern. It has to do with what drives us, what interests us, what frightens us, what satisfies us. It has to do with what I want and what, if any role you play in my not getting what I want. If I can believe that you are, in some way involved in opposing my forward motion, preventing my success and acquisitions then you become my enemy and that places me in a combat role. To go beyond you and ultimately get what I want, I have to eliminate the threat that you imply and defeat your efforts to block me.

That was one of the most emphasized lessons we were given as children. We were carefully taught that someone is always getting in the way of what we want. Winning is everything. There are a number of maneuvers and manipulations that we can learn, practice and refine that will provide us with the tools of "being right" and "winning" at the game of life.

It is primarily within the home environment in which we grow up that the belief systems, habits and behaviors of our parents and mentors are transferred to us. It is with the repetition of their teachings and the pressure to perform accordingly, that we develop our commitment to fulfilling their expectations and we do so to assure their good will and acceptance of us. To fail in this compliance role usually means that we will be subjected to the withholding of love, approval and full participation in the family group.

It's sort of the "monkey see, monkey do" syndrome. We mimic the lessons that our parents model. We repeat the mantras of fear that they utter about the world and its people and adopt the defenses that they employ to keep danger at a distance. Collectively these behaviors led us to believe that people "out there" are fearsome, are threatening to us and, for our safety, need to be kept separate from ourselves. We construct elaborate thoughts about just how separate they need to be and why we have to avoid them to stay safe. As long as we see them as separate from us and believe they can be harmful, we are compelled to resist, oppose, and even fight back just to establish a modicum of safety. We launch an attack/counter-attack syndrome and with each of our assaults, we engender more fear in those we oppose and invite their best efforts to do us in.

The wheels are off the track. In fact we aren't even sure where the track has gone. Where does the anger, the fear, the attack mentality come from. Why are we seemingly always pitted against those around us? Where do we pick up the beliefs about the threats, danger and perils that we have to deal with? It's obvious that to return to saner living, to establish some measure of peace and to reduce the mayhem that surrounds us, we have to understand the sources of the challenges and the conflicts that we're constantly embroiled in. We have to truly get to the basics of how humans interact in order to address the enmity that is always at hand.

The old saw about fight or flight is ever present. Its presence suggests that either way, fighting or running from the opposition leaves us in a very insecure status. It also raises the question as to whether it is even possible to live with others in any semblance of getting along. Even those that we regard as closest to us are among the active disrupters of our relationships.

Marital pairs, parents and children, friends and neighbors, bosses and employees, are frequently at odds and in conflict with one another about intellectual and emotional differences. Evening table talk at home is replete with accounts of the day's unresolved challenges and the negative emotional states that arise from our frustrations. Coffee klatches are loaded with animated discussions about someone's slight or insult or stupidity. The world is inundated with negative issues and responses. It all leads to counter charges, character assassination, criticism, projection of opinions onto others and thinly veiled talk about repercussions for hurts and inconsideration.

Each face-off is a mini war and generates more negative energy that never seems to dissipate. Loaded emotional situations sow seeds of future negative harvests.

A major question: What has to happen for each of us to be convinced of the folly of continuing to live this way? What would it take to lay down our jealousies, our meanness, our blaming, shaming and accusing others? Haven't we seen enough yet to realize that it is not only ineffective to treat each other this way, but it is leading to an un-imaginable way of living in the near future as it continues to escalate in severity?

Here is a partial listing of the problems we face in today's world.

- Immorality
- Pedophilia
- Rape
- Obsession with sexuality
- Untruths in every area of our lives
- Cheating, stealing
- Marital infidelity
- Misrepresenting issues to others
- Lying that happens in every venue
- Manipulating others for self gain
- Churches that are failing their congregations
- Unscrupulous business practices that wreck corporations and assault employees
- Lusting for all forms of power against and over others
- Prurient entertainment
- Shallowness of interpersonal relationships
- Character assassination of others for personal gain

- Derogation of each other for personal gain
- Lack of commitment to decency, integrity, truth, openness
- Misrepresenting truth for personal gain
- Personal physical abuse leading to unhealthy life styles
- Unthinking destruction of the planet and its resources
- Failing to provide appropriate nurture, lessons and support for our young
- False, untruthful advertising to misrepresent products, etc.
- Distortions of truth for political gain
- Avoidance of commitment to essential practices for harmonious living
- Consciously exposing others to harmful practices
- Ridiculing others for their involvement in decent and honest endeavors
- Not teaching appropriate behaviors and truths to young people
- Not challenging inappropriate behavior and not attempting to correct it
- Not sharing concern for practices that are obviously harmful
- Not fostering appropriate spirituality for all and supporting others in their search
- Not offering our support, help and acceptance of others trying to improve their lives

This comprehensive listing of the ills of our society is overwhelming. It will continue to expand until any semblance of a decent society will be gone. It is up to us who harbor grave concern over this plight to commit to and stay with an effective effort to reverse the process and restore our collective selves to the life that is and has always been available to us.

In America, as great as we have been, we are in a position for a sliding decline in all aspects of our culture simply because our wonderful blessings of affluence and power have made us careless, apathetic, unwilling to be aware of the dangers that are in our midst and most of all, unwilling to make major changes in our life-styles in order to preserve the rich heritage our ancestors gave to us. Look at the indifference the nation and its leaders display when confronted with personal and public behaviors that are the testimony of our declining value system. No one cares and we become more apathetic each day.

Each of us is so busy with **"ME", "Mine" and "Ours"**, that we have no time or energy to devote to the rebuilding of our culture for **"all of us"**.

As a practicing Psychiatrist in the 60's and 70's I first became interested not only in the individual pathology that people presented but beyond that to the impact that it was having on the family, community, national and planetary structures. Nothing has stemmed the tide of selfishness and dysfunction since that time. In fact, there has been a steady erosion of quality in all of our collective enterprises since then. *"The decline of a nation does begin in the homes of its people."* And people from those homes take their greed, their apathy and their lack of commitment to values into their jobs and societal relationships so their contagious attitudes and behaviors have reached epidemic proportions. We have a full-blown plague going on here in America, the Beautiful.

The purpose of this book is to ask you to join me in looking at the way we fail to teach our young a sense of grand purpose, a set of values, a commitment to excellence and the thrill of an accomplished life. Instead, we consistently instill shabby value systems in our young, fail to teach them enduring and enriching lessons, and use fear to program them to conform and fit into a society that is dangerously near demise.

We have failed to realize that the procreation of a human child starts an obligation to commit to that child for the next two decades our best loving care, protection, support, and encouragement to assure that that individual receives an optimal chance for fulfillment in his/her lifetime. Each child needs the same period of time and nurture for a fair chance to attain their potential.

Only our children can be the dreamers of wonder for the future. Only they can be the integrators of plans and dreams that can restore America to its place of prominence and leadership for the rest of the world. Only our proper teaching of children in our homes can replace the wretched examples they see each day in our public personages. Only a massive commitment to positive change in the way we train our young can develop the next generation into the leaders and doers that can prevent the American culture from joining with the Persians, the Greeks, the Romans, the British Empire and others who failed to heed the clarion calls to change their ways.

This book attempts to look at how our adult beliefs, expectations, assumptions and attitudes developed in our own early lives. It points out that all of these adult concepts that we choose, decide and act upon each day were originally only the thoughts from the minds of our parents, who got them from their parents, who got them from their parents–ad infinitum. It's a sort of "hand-me-down" casual treatment of a vital and necessary process for developing effective human beings.

In the collection of thoughts and beliefs that you carry around in your head each day, there are precious few that were original thoughts on your part. You, like all of us were expected to absorb the collective "thinking stuff" from family, school, and society and to behave in ways that reflected how well you learned the lessons. How could you become creative, happy or free when you were absorbed in doing what family and society shoved down your throat as _"the way it has to be"_?

It's time to wake up, realize you have been conned into being what you are and that you have the divine right (and responsibility) to change it in any way that is necessary to become more creative, more effective and more joyful. It's your life. Take it out of the museum and begin to live it.

14

CHAPTER 3

HOW DID IT ALL HAPPEN?

What if our parents had been all loving, all knowing, and all supportive while they were raising us? What if they had understood the makeup of the human brain and its thinking mechanisms and the role that their teaching played in how we developed the beliefs and attitudes that will determine the quality of our journey for the rest of our lives?

What if they had been able to look forward in time and visualize a picture of us (their children) fully developed in regard to our God-given potential and had predicated their teachings, lessons, examples, and role-modeling on concepts and ideas that would be necessary to assure our growing into that image? What if the lessons they received from their parents (that have kept them constricted and limited during their own life time) had been excluded from our programming? Instead, if they had taken the negatives and the fear out of the process of socializing us, there would have been more room for love, support, patience, understanding and forgiveness assuring that we would become truly functional and enlightened persons.

Suppose they had been more concerned with the task of shaping young minds for illustrious, fulfilling futures rather than simply teaching us the restrictive things that would socialize us to "fit into society"? Suppose they had put aside the

petty differences that so often became soul–shaking battles for control, for power and retribution within the family and had tried to instill in us a sense of exhilaration and adventure for breaking out of the constraints and limitations that social-ization alone produces?

Suppose they had had all the patience and love that was necessary to nurture us along the journey of growing up to adulthood and then had had the wisdom to help us achieve independent living without instilling feelings of fear, shame and guilt?

What unnecessary criticism, censure, degradation, physical punishment, guilt-production, and feelings of worthlessness could have been avoided in your life if your parents had only known more about how the human mind works?

How would you be different today if all this had been true?

It is like the well-known adage about computers: "Garbage in – Garbage Out". Whatever a computer is programmed with determines the scope and limits of the effectiveness of that particular computer. The same is true of human brains. The quality of the multiple training inputs during our growth and development determines the quality of our ability to learn, to act, to grow, and to cope effectively with the variety of experiences that will continue to impact us throughout life.

We need to understand that these concepts that constitute our own **"belief system"** today were originally nothing more than the "be-liefs" that our parents learned from their ancestors. Those beliefs that were part of early life learning weren't necessarily true, many were badly flawed, others were total distortions of the way things really are. However those lessons were forced on and stored in our parents' subconscious minds as **"the way it is"**. Our parents have spent their lives living according to those inherited but flawed beliefs, assump-tions and expectations that were mandated by their own parents and with that set of beliefs that they had to adopt to keep peace in their young days, reaped the consequences of behaving according to <u>limiting paradigms.</u>

Subsequently they passed them on to us in our early years as the"gospel" for our lives. Today we are conducting our lives according to this information that was handed down to us and therefore we are subject to similar limitations, prejudices, and constrictions that were embedded in the belief systems of our programmers.

Some of these beliefs do represent an accurate and workable view of issues but many more of these acquired notions have become self-limiting constraints that keep us from fuller and more effective living. We've grown so used to the limits that we accept them as <u>"what is possible for me".</u>

Have we inadvertently passed the same materials to our younger generation and perpetuated the body of myths and half-truths for their lives?

Many observers of human behavior have suggested that the average person is operating on only 10-20% of their human potential; that the remainder of their possibilities are locked up in the fears, the disbeliefs, and the shortstops that are contained in those programmed teachings. What could you do if you took possession of the remaining 80% of your capability? We must learn to open our minds to that reserve potential and clearly see how we, ourselves, have created our limits by adopting the limiting beliefs of our predecessors.

For those of you who were fortunate enough to have had mature, caring parents who gave you love, support, recognition and encouragement in your young years, you avoided much negative input and arrived at adulthood better prepared to stretch for your potential. Those of you who have been given dysfunctional and discouraging lessons in early life have larger and higher hurdles to jump but you have the right and the power to make life from this point on, whatever you dream of and commit to pursue. It's not too late!

Because of the pervasive and inappropriate preparation of our young for the vicissitudes of life, the world is presently chaotic and disintegrating. We spend much of our time and effort exploring basic and core questions searching for answers that our current mindsets can't explain:

- Why does the world seem to be breaking up?

- Why have values, integrity, honesty and respect disappeared?

- Why are so many of our systems falling apart?

- Why are many wars in far off places having an impact on life here at home?

- Why do famine, evil and sadness prevail?

- Why are so many innocents becoming victims?

- Why is this scenario taking place in a world that was designed for and capable of providing abundance for everyone?

In large measure it is because of **my** selfishness, **my** greed, **my** jealousy, **my** mean-spiritedness, **my** abuses of others, **my** choosing to use fear to control others, **my** thoughtlessness—plus **yours, and yours, and yours.** Collectively we are psychological and emotional wrecks trying to interact as adults using concepts that were originally taught in an aura of fear and designed to keep kids clean, quiet and out of the way. Rules designed for control of children cannot be effective in developing adults to be anything but angry child-people, incapable of facing adult challenges effectively and joyfully.

When I indulge in mean-spiritedness, it begets the same from you and others. We truly mirror one another. We respond in kind and as long as we spew out negative thoughts and emotions, they are reflected back. When enough negativity is expressed in the world, there is little room to experience what the world was designed for, namely, abundance, peace, loving relationships, empathy, and sharing. The more the negative specter dominates our behavioral patterns, the more it seems the natural way to live and the more it will eclipse the potential paradise that life was meant to be.

Because you have chosen to explore this book, I'm going to request that, while you are perusing its content, that you **"go out of your mind"**; out of your "everyday mind" that is saddled with limiting and constricting beliefs, prejudice and negative attitudes. As long as you are thinking the same thoughts, doing the same things, you will predictably get the same results and outcomes, which you are desirous to do something about and change.

The timeworn axioms are still relevant:

"If you always do what you've always done
You'll always get what you've always gotten."
"If there's no <u>change</u>, there's no change."

I realize that you can't (nor, at this point, should you try to) eradicate your current set of thoughts, beliefs and paradigms on which you base your actions. I am merely asking that you suspend your reliance on them and open up your thinking to new notions that can set you free and expand your performance.

This sounds like a monumental, if not impossible task but only because you have never considered it could happen for you personally. If you could learn the set of beliefs that you currently have absorbed from childhood to the present, you can now consciously learn to sort them out, discard those that are holding you back and develop a new set of thought habits. The cost is personal effort and the reward is that of personal freedom.

Is this attempt for growth only for your own benefit? Certainly not! In today's world where over 50% of marriages end in divorce and a significant number of the marriages that stay together are in constant conflict, there is a pervasive climate for childrearing that is not conducive for children reaching their full potential. Unless we have a critical mass of people willing to radically change how they operate in everyday life, and unless those enhanced beliefs and expectations are promulgated into the successive generations, our destiny and that of our progeny will be a worsening picture.

At this point, I should interject that if you really are <u>totally satisfied</u> with the way things are for you in you're:

- Private life

- Work Life

- Social life

- Financial situation

- Educational level

- Creativity

- Relational life

- Marital and love life

- And in the way the world is currently performing-

You should put the book down and go about your regular routines.

For those of you who are remaining on the journey, you are going to learn that your thoughts, belief system, and actions should be brought under your conscious and intelligent control at all times. The alternative is what you struggle with now. Your life and current reality are being caused by and subject to the control of unconscious dictates that you learned a long time ago to please others and to avoid punishment and rejection. You have simply failed to update your knowledge base in reaching adulthood.

Your **"Current Reality"** is the conglomeration of all the experiences (results) that emanate from your choices, decisions, and actions on a daily basis.

It includes:

- What you have (or do not have).

- What work and leisure you engage in.

- Who your family, friends, and associates are.

- What the quality of your relationships with them is.

- Whether you are manifesting your true potential / talents.

- Or whether you are struggling against the forces you believe are arresting your progress and success.

Current Reality is also:

- How you deal with joy and disappointment.

- How you deal with emotions.

  ★ Your own emotions.

  ★ Emotions of others toward you.

- How you handle power.

- How you cope with challenges.

- How you deal with conflict when it arises.

- How you express love and affection.

- How you receive love and affection.

- How you sort through and manage the feelings associated with your every day living.

- Your willingness to give, receive and share in adult ways.

In summary, your **"Current Reality"** is all about your behavior in all aspects of your daily living. If you are unhappy with any aspect of your life that you are presently experiencing and want to make changes, you have the innate potential to design whatever lifestyle you desire but there are a few things to remember:

- You can't really change anyone else, only yourself

- Only they can make lasting changes in themselves. Don't waste your and their time trying to alter others.

- The same is true for those who presently would like to change you.

- There is a potential risk in making positive personal changes to improve your own future.

  * You will no longer be satisfied with your current reality.

  * You might anger, disappoint, and irritate others in your life and relationships will change because of it.

  * It could get lonely for you as your growth leaves them behind

- It will take much time and great effort to break out of your current patterns and during the journey you might revert to the "old ways" temporarily.

- You must get back on track and persist in the new behavior to make the new dreams come true.

- If you are successful in this first effort to cause the change that you want, recognize that you will be repeating this action countless times during your lifespan in traveling from your "current realities" to loftier and more satisfying experiences. You will be replacing your current limited lifestyle with a new way of seeing and experiencing this wonderful world in which we live.

The acronym "**P-BAR**" has been developed as a tool to assist you in the first step of expanding your awareness of how you have personally developed. It can be thought of as a sort of formula to use in discovering how we grew from infants into adulthood and how we acquired our belief systems. Before anything can change in your life, you must first become totally aware of who you are, what you hold as truths, why you do things the way you do, where and how you put together the accumulation of beliefs, assumptions, expectations, attitudes and habits that control your current living. This is where **P-BAR** comes in.

Only when you clearly understand your present status will you be in a position to consciously design how you want it to be different.

The next chapter will open up the **P-BAR** concept to begin your own liberation from the archaic rules of our ancestors and the way society wants you to "fit the mold."

CHAPTER 4

WHAT IS P-BAR?

P-BAR is an acronym for the process that all of us traverse in growing from infancy to adulthood. As you grow more familiar with its significance, you will be in a stronger position to understand how you got to be whatever you see yourself to be at the present time.

P = Programming What we have been taught and learned.
B = Beliefs Interpretations we formed out of those lessons.
A = Action How our current actions are based on our belief system.
R = Results The consequences that arise from our actions.

It is a formulistic way to see what you were taught and learned as "truth" and how that makes you strong or vulnerable as the case may be. It is the beginning of understanding where you got the ideas and paradigms that you are using in living everyday life. It will clarify why you don't always do the things that could alter your life forever.

Reasons for working with this information:

- To understand the learning process that took you from infancy to your current adulthood thinking.

- To discover current beliefs and assumptions that are <u>ineffective</u> for you and prevent your personal growth.

- To show you how to activate your potential capabilities for growth, however limited you might feel at the moment.

By understanding what your programming process consisted of, (rules you were given by well-meaning but misinformed or ignorant mentors), you then can:

- Discard beliefs that no longer work and substitute new beliefs that can win for you.

- Create a new wide-open path toward self-fulfillment.

- Develop new levels of effective performance and outcomes.

- Release your current limitations forever.

- Increase satisfaction by discarding those impediments to growth.

- Replace them with more effective ways of manifesting your innate and latent wisdom and talent.

Memorize the **P-B-A-R** acronym and use it to reconstruct the processes that you were exposed to in growing up, recognizing how it originally formed the model by which you currently live in limitation. You will then be in a position to redesign power beliefs to replace faulty concepts from your programming and move into expanded futures.

CHAPTER 5

PROGRAMMING

Today's world is a complicated mess defined by the many diverse and conflictual issues that we are inundated with simultaneously.

There are many wars of varying sizes that are going on around the world. There is violence in every venue you can imagine: the home, the streets, our corporations, our societal groups, our educational institutions, road rage on the highways, gang actions everywhere, rape, and broad-based crime waves across the nation. Our sporting events are peppered with fan encounters, riots over the scoring outcomes, burning and pillaging over popular victories in major sports, sport stars that are involved in rapes, drugs, pedophilia, murders, and fans attacking officials on the fields.

Some of those issues are of our own making, predicated distortions of the **"programming"** that we received as youngsters growing up. Over time, we have rather lost track of just how poorly we were prepared by our parents and significant other mentors for the challenge of dealing with life processes. Over time we came to believe that mess in which we live was "the way it was meant to be".

Many of the lessons we were given for living were simply hackneyed hand-me-down concepts from our parent's own early life experiences and resulted in a perpetuation of the limited and ineffective life styles that their parents and mentors had imbedded in their own psyches.

During our growing-up period, all of us were subjected to countless admonitions, lessons, rules, do's and don'ts, rights and wrongs, advice and demands about many things from our elders. These became mandates that we felt compelled to adopt and ultimately, through repetition and practice, they actually became elements of our own "belief system" which determines how we think, how we see the world, what we expect is possible or impossible for us and what gives shape to our own sense of self-worth and self-esteem.

Initially, in our early days when we were small and defenseless we were not in a position to challenge the quality, wisdom or accuracy of the lessons. For the sake of approval, acceptance, avoiding punishment and being loved we assumed a need to learn and employ the concepts as they were taught. In the learning process they became stored in our subconscious as "truths", "standard operation procedures" and essential behaviors for us to operate by if we wanted full acceptance in the adult world.

Our expectations, our assumptions and the outcomes of our living became dependent on the quality and effectiveness of our "programming" which was then stored for readiness for our unconscious mind to use. Once the "rules of the road" were engraved in our belief system, we automatically acted in accordance with those beliefs and, depending on the quality and appropriateness of our paradigms we reaped either effective, good, successful behavior and outcomes or we continued to flounder and fail because of negative and unsupporting beliefs about ourselves emanating from the people who taught us.

Countless people today are trying desperately to attain goals, successful outcomes and meaningful relationships in their lives by applying the inaccurate, derogatory, and self-defeating attitudes and principles that they adopted from parents and mentors as children. Their sense of self-worth and self-esteem is so shabby that they can't visualize themselves in any successful endeavors.

Over the ages, most people have accepted the limitations, the frustrations, and the negative beliefs of their **"programming"**, feeling that there is nothing that can be different for them. They believe they are **"stuck"** at the places they were **taught to be "stuck" at.** They miss out on the joy and excitement that comes with engaging in and succeeding at life's challenges. Because they believe in failure, that is what they find. What you **"see"** and **"expect"** is what you end up getting. But it can all be changed and we will get to that.

They are convinced by the propaganda along the way that desirable outcomes and happiness are *not in the cards for them.* They are hung up on untrue common thought paradigms that say *"it's too late to change, too hard to learn something new", "that you are behaving in ways that will never let you win or succeed"* and they believe those lies with a passion.

The truth of the matter is that the things you had to learn were mostly wrong and when you examine the content of those many lessons, you can easily see the wrongness in them that you couldn't see or know about as a child. You can see that the quality and content of the lessons was predominantly negative and disparaging, but again, when you were small there was no chance of successfully challenging the programmers or refusing to capitulate to the parental power.

As indelible and entrenched as our beliefs, expectations and assumptions appear to be, in reality they are <u>**only thoughts, words and stories passed on to us**</u> by well-meaning but often ignorant, frustrated and limited parents, extended family, teachers and others. They aren't necessarily the real "truth" but only archaic and habituated ways of blindly getting through life day after day. And, being just thoughts and societal myths, they can be changed to anything we want them to be in our lives. We are not obliged to carry that kind of **"junk"** to our graves simply because we learned it from older and once-controlling people in our lives.

The <u>real purpose</u> of parents in the scheme of things is to get us through the early stage when we, of necessity, are dependent and unprepared and then hand the reins of OUR life over to us as we move toward independence and subsequently a later stage of interdependence with mature society.

Unwittingly in the process of raising kids, they failed to allow the child appropriate room to experiment, to fail and subsequently to try again without humiliation and to experience the fullness of trial-error-and correction methods that would grow stronger kids and teach stronger values along the way.

Most parents don't know when to quit. Their own insecure self-image and sense of purpose requires them to remain in dominant, controlling and often incarcerating roles that smother children's emergence into fully productive lives. It is difficult for parents to accept the thought that their offspring can do well without their riding herd on their lives. The **"empty-nest"** syndrome plagues many parents and because they feel it justifies their continued control, they pose great obstacles to the further growth and skill development of their children

Common childhood lessons: (Look at the predominant negativity)

Don't.........

Don't touch things

Don't cry

Leave things alone

Don't pout

Don't hit

Don't break.........

Don't sulk

Don't lie to me

Don't talk to me that way

Don't get dirty

Don't play with yourself

Don't run away—leave the yard

Don't fight with your sister

Don't take other people's things

Don't steal

Don't talk dirty

Don't forget...........

Pay attention to what I'm telling you

Don't play in the street

Don't go next door

Don't ever go into my desk

Don't put that in your mouth

Don't leave the lights on

Don't make noise

Don't leave your toys out

Don't spill

Don't make a mess

Don't look at me like that

Don't kick.........me, the dog, etc

Don't sing now at the table

Don't pound on the piano

Don't pull up the flowers

Don't argue

Don't ever do that again

Don't talk about the family to others

Don't bother daddy, mommy

Come straight home = don't delay or be late

Don't mark the walls, furniture

Don't touch the computer

Don't let me catch you doing that again

Did you hear what I said?

Stay out of_____don't go there

Don't interrupt when big people are talking

Don't touch daddy's papers

Don't repeat that

Don't ask!

Don't touch it—you might break it

Don't do as I do—do as I say

Don't you question me.

You're too young to know, to decide, to do that

You'll never, (always)..............

Get that look off your face

Wipe that smile off your face or I'll wipe it off for you

Stop the crying or I'll give you something to cry about

I'm so ashamed of you, disappointed in you, angry with, upset with you

Who do you think you are?

What were you thinking?

What's gotten into you?

Why did you do that?

What will people think of you?

If you ever do that again, you'll be sorry

Good boys don't do those things. (You did it therefore you are bad)

You don't get to go

No circus for you buddy

Ask yourself, did you like that kind of stuff when you were little and growing up?

No? Then why would you think it is appropriate and acceptable to your own children? Be conscious and vigilant about how you teach and talk in order to avoid contaminating this generation in the same manner that you were taught.

What are we trying to set up in the mind of the child with these types of declarations?

- That they are small and dependent

- That we are in charge and don't forget it

- That they are wrong and need to be told

- That they can get into "our kind of trouble" if they misbehave

- That in this house "that" doesn't fly

- That they are out of line

- That they aren't lovable or acceptable at the moment.

- That these are the house rules—no exceptions

- Trying to package our own expectations for them to learn and adopt

- Teach them "right" and "wrong" (But by whose standards?)

- Keep them from behaving in ways that reflect on us as parents

- Keep them under control

- Keep them clean, quiet and out of the way.

- Keep them from trespassing on our adult "rights"

What we are really doing is transferring all the rules, prohibitions, expectations and assumptions that we were taught as children to them. Usually our parents (the grandparents) are there looking on and expecting us to pass it on. If we forget, they will remind us of our own failures with our own children according to their beliefs).

This is the **obsession of society**; that we have to perpetuate the same rules down through the ages. It's a lot like hell week at the fraternity or sorority where last year you were initiated painfully and now it is your turn to inflict pain on others.

The most dominant results of such childrearing tactics are:

- Resentment in the child

- Their finding creative ways to resist or disobey

- Humiliation of the child with a sense of internal shame

- Depriving them of lessons that would teach effective coping skills

- Failing to develop thoughts of unconditional love and closeness in the family

- Missed opportunities for rich and fulfilling experiences for the children

All the time we are passing the above along to our kids, we are missing many opportunities to teach them the real and truly effective ways for successful and productive lives. We are also perpetuating the model of society that prevents full and empowering energy into the lives of the younger generation.

Currently I am working with groups of chronically depressed adults who have failed at all of the challenges of life; the successful jobs, loving relationships, a sense of personal fulfillment, a feeling of having contributed to our culture, of developing a history of having explored and savored the best that our world has to offer. In hearing their stories of how it all started and unfolded for them, they could write the textbooks on <u>what not to do</u> in early preparatory years of teaching children about life. We need to unearth the practices that are fostering deprived childhoods and replace those age-old ways with <u>love-driven</u> approaches to initiating children into membership in this wondrous and unlimited world.

It could start very simply by abandoning the critical, punitive, shaming, humiliating, emotionally rejecting approaches toward children and THINKING, really THINKING about what kind of lessons, treatment, loving, forgiving, sharing, mutually experiencing, nurturing, encouraging experiences would best enrich a young growing human being?

There has to be a willingness to put aside your own adult comfort, interests, pastimes, and indulgences in order to give the highly touted (but mostly missing) **"quality time"** to the process of ushering children through early years to a full blown young adulthood that is rich in loving memories, of shared experiences, of parenting that was thoughtfully committed to maximizing growth potential. And keep in mind that when you produce a newborn, you have a commitment of two decades to that and each subsequent child to see them through the appropriate growing period.

Real Lessons (Could begin with and include, but not limited to the following parental attitudes in reaching out to)

- You are inherently a good human being with an archetype inside that knows how you should really grow and learn.

- You are young, inexperienced, and eager to learn in a loving atmosphere about the issues of life. You have to be shown the paths to exploration and have adults rejoice in your discoveries. We will make that happen for you.

- You are, at the outset, a cellular combination of your father and mother's DNA and are destined to maximize the beauty and effectiveness of what you are designed to be.

- You are not bad when your curiosity prods you to explore your environment and you are still clumsy.

- You are not bad when you try to cope with relationships in ways that need guidance. That guidance must be done in love and understanding about (not the moment's preference of behavior but rather) how we want you to really learn the practices of effective interaction in the world.

- You are not bad when you begin to realize that the perpetrators of the lessons for your own behavior are often guilty of the same or worse behaviors themselves. We have learning to do also.

- You are not bad when you discover there are double standards and we must try to work that out together as parent and child.

- You are not bad when you try to negotiate the insertion of our rules on situations that seem unfair. (Those feelings of unfairness in early days are carried as resentments, humiliations, guilt, and depreciated self-esteem the rest of our lives.)

- The world is a beautiful place with abundance for all. You are intended to find its love, its peace, and its acceptance and to be a part of the mechanism that passes it on to succeeding generations. Let's explore together until you really understand the whole picture.

- The world is driven by love, not fear, encouragement not limitations, expansiveness not contraction.

- You are already creative, whole and resourceful.

Our parents got their "stuff" from ancestors in the same way we received ours from our parents. They received no help in altering and correcting their programming, their illusions, and their stumbling blocks. These are societal, cultural, tribal beliefs often times perpetuated by individuals purposefully trying to stymie change and keep people dependent, limited and under wraps.

Most of us cling to the early life programming, not because it is effective but rather because it is familiar, "safe", requires no risky effort to change and—because it makes us like the majority, we minimize criticism and rejection. We also buy it because it is the price of being loved and accepted. But what a price to pay.

Changing involves something **"different"** and different implies something **new**, something that might not go well at first, might be embarrassing, might even fail but without changing we continue in our constrained and limited fashion. That way the world will continue as it has for centuries, repeating the stupid and ineffective practices that keep a limited and failing civilization struggling against issues of our own making.

Check back to the listing of common Programming statements. While some families did it "right", the majority of parents were never enlightened as to what programming should be and therefore simply duplicated their own experience for the next generation. It should also be mentioned that the children who undergo the programming in the home of origin, also, unwittingly contribute to the distortion of the lessons and admonitions when they add their own misinterpretations to what is being said and done to them.

It is time for monumental changes in the way we relate to and perpetuate the human race. To fail to meet that challenge would be the greatest failure of our species and will further the deterioration of planetary existence.

Are you willing to help bring about family and societal change?

CHAPTER 6

REFLECTIONS ON YOUR "PROGRAMMING"

At this point let's take the time to return to your own childhood days and recall the salient aspects of what your programming was like. I know that it was a long time ago for many of you but it will be time well spent to better understand the various impacts that shaped your life (and may still be active in driving your choices and behavior.) So, referring back to the last chapter on *"Programming"* use the information to examine your own early days as a child and adolescent to focus on what you have clung to.

I would remind you that for most people, their current adult behaviors are a **"knee jerk"** reaction that happens automatically in response to events and is not something that you have to think out with each event. You learned to develop fixed ways of responding to a whole variety of circumstances and challenges that life presented and, once you had a "workable" (for you) coping mechanism for handling any specific situation, you carefully stored it into your subconscious mind from which location it is ready and willing to rise to the occasion when called upon.

We developed these "fixed" responses because it is economically advantageous to have a series of quick and ready answers to deal with the daily array of things that come up. If we had to stop and design an answer for each issue and for each occurrence of the issue as they arose, we would be less able to get through an average day. But, as convenient as it might be to have fast, automatic responses to situations, I think you can also see that it commits us to habitual and often inflexible behaviors and reduces the variety of options for us to use. I also think when you have the people of your daily experiences (family members, co-workers, acquaintances, and special relationships) meeting with their collective storehouses of their set responses, it reduces the spontaneity and flavor of personal interactions. You know and your friends know precisely how to expect you to be in given encounters and it is the sum of those patterns that defines your "personality".

Bear in mind that in your own beginnings you were an infant with no history, no knowledge of the world, vulnerable and defenseless and in that state you were exposed to the environment of the home with all its positive and negative overtones already developed and active in the family constellation.

In looking back at the early days of your childhood, I would pose a series of questions for your consideration. Your willingness to react to these questions will most likely shed some understanding to the flavor of those times.

What was the emotional tone of the home?

- Warm, loving, safe and welcoming or noisy, harsh, cold and scary.

- What people were present in those days?

- Were you the first born or were there other siblings already there?

- What parent was most present in those early days?

- Were there extended family members there also? (Grandparents, in-laws)

What were your earliest memories of being part of that family?

- A lot of touching and holding?

- A lot of noise and unpleasant sounds?

- Being alone much of the time?

I can recall an early experience of being on a swing, falling out and getting a mouth full of sand that was scary. I also remember playing with my father who had given me a train set. I date that to my third year of life because that was the time my father died and the end of his influence and presence in my life.

I know we moved to a different place (the town of my mother's childhood) and recall how stiff and cold it seemed where everything was so unloving and unwelcoming. I began to feel it was not happy for my mother either. She was sad and appeared troubled. Let me add here that these thoughts were three-year old feelings and were more emotional that factual but still were the earliest impacts of events on my mind where all of this was being stored.

I recall my first real booboo that I felt guilty about. On the stairway in the back of the house there was a can of unpopped popcorn on the top step. In my investigating the can, it tumbled down the stairs emptying is contents from top to bottom of the stairs and that was the first time I recall being scolded and made to feel at "bad" and at fault.

So what were some of your earliest memories, either pleasant or unpleasant that left a lasting impression on you?

As they come to mind, write them down lest then go underground again. All of the events and experiences of those days were imprinted into your subconscious mind and in one way or another became influences in your memory bank.

Which parent was the dominant force in your early days?
Which one would you go to for solace?

Which one for advice?

Which parent was most likely to play with you or to read to you?

Who was best at comforting you when scared or hurt?

What elements of the extended family were prominent in your childhood?

What was the interaction between your parents?

Loving or quarreling?

What were their fights about?

When they had an argument or a spat, how did that make you feel?

Were they severe enough that you felt someone would get hurt?

Did anyone ever get hurt in such encounters?

What vacations did the family take? What do you recall about them?

Where did you go on vacations?

Which were your favorite vacations? Which ones did you not like?

What were holidays like?

How about Thanksgiving, Christmas, Easter, Hanukkah, the Fourth of July

What about your school experiences?

What were the early days of your schooling like? Was it scary or exciting?

What teachers stand out in your past?

What were recess and the playground like? Threatening or fun?

How did you feel about gym class?

What were your favorite subjects? Your least favorite subjects?

How were your grades in elementary, middle and high school?

What were the educational backgrounds of your parents? Older siblings?

What were your parent's attitudes about your schooling?

Were they involved with PTA and other school functions for you?

How were your family relationships with the neighbors?
  Was there a neighborhood character that stood out?
  Was it a safe neighborhood or were there difficulties and challenges?

Did you ever run away from home? For what reason(s)?

What were the family's spiritual beliefs and patterns like?

What groups did you become part of in childhood and adolescence?
  Church groups, Scouts, Campfire Girls, Other?

What sports did you most enjoy? Which ones were you best at?

What were your family's attitudes about life issues?
  What did you learn about money?
  What were you taught about patriotism?
  What lessons were you given about fairness and honesty?

What was the most frightening experience of your growing up?

What were family attitudes about elderly, impoverished people?

What experiences and lessons about racial and gender differences?

What was the most exciting thing to happen in your growing up?
  What disappointments did you experience?
  What would you like to have had different about your growing up?

Who was the most influential person in your developmental years?

When you started to formulate dreams and wishes for your life, what were they?

What early ideas did you have about careers, further education and personal development?

Did any of them happen for you the way you wanted it to be?

Did you have heroes and heroines that you wanted to emulate?

Who were they?

This kind of recapitulation about earlier times can serve you in a number of ways. Many of those early life experiences have had a profound effect on your emotional and psychological development. When you were young and inexperienced, a lot of issues appeared to be frightening, exciting, stimulating or repressive because of our as-yet underdeveloped thought processes in childhood. We often put our own inaccurate evaluations, attributions or interpretations on issues that arose in our early life. But if you have continued to hold the subconscious impressions of early days they may have become part of your "baggage" that is still troublesome in adulthood today.

I urge you to spend some time reviewing what your "programming" was like. How much of what your parents passed on to you was simply their trying to fulfill a vague responsibility to shape you as they had been shaped in their day by their parents who had been trained in an earlier generation. How much influence of those early rules and lessons still plague your efforts to be more free and open to be yourself?

So, now let's move to our **"B"** **(Belief)** segment and continue on the journey.

CHAPTER 7

BELIEFS ("B")

Where do we get our beliefs from? It has been suggested that the source of beliefs lies in the preponderance of the Programming content that we, as children assimilate during the early years of our socialization. Don Miguel Ruiz, the author of ***"The Four Agreements"*** also calls Programming the process of **domesticating** our young, not dissimilar to the reward / punishment style used in training our pets. In the growing up process the majority of children are subjected to daily lessons, criticisms, and accusations and labeling from the parental side. As already alluded to in Chapter 6, the predominantly negative tone of programming as it is practiced is the foundation for impaired self-images and self-esteem in children. The collections of statements and inputs from parents create kids who have dysfunctional ideas about themselves and those shaming and humiliating experiences give distorted content to their psyches.

The beliefs that children formulate about themselves are constructs built out of negative and distorted programming that is assimilated into their subconscious mind where it is then the unconscious autopilot for their future life.

Definition of "belief": That which is believed; an accepted opinion; conviction of truth or reality

Synonyms for Belief ("B")

- "Truth".

- Assumptions.

- Expectations.

- Prejudices.

- Attitudes.

- Habits.

- Prohibitions.

- Filters – What my mind allows to enter or screens out.

- My "autopilot"

- My "blind spots"

- My Ego

We've begun to see how the programming content in our earliest years was learned, stored in our unconscious and was converted into word symbols listed above that constitute our **"Belief System" ("B")**.

My Belief System includes <u>all</u> of the inputs I have absorbed during my lifetime.

- The good and the bad.

- The positive and negative.

- The true and false.

- The kind and unkind.

- The supportive and the undermining.

- The factual and the unsubstantiated.

In our process of growing up, we were subjected to the lessons, experiences and the inputs from any adults who were close enough to us to have influence on our learning. These original thoughts and bits of information were not of our own discovery, nor necessarily true and viable, but were the **"hand-me-down"** accumulated knowledge that was in the minds of our programmers. It was all that they had to go on and we were supposed to **"get it"** from them, keep it and eventually pass the same "stuff" to our kids. That way we would be guaranteeing consistency for how to fit into society and its expectations of us and to maintain consistency from generation to generation.

<u>In those early days when we were:</u>

- Small

- Frightened

- Uninformed

- Defenseless

- Unquestioning

- Vulnerable

It was mostly a wise thing to accept whatever incoming information flowed to us. In most instances, if we questioned or rebelled or declined to indicate our acceptance of it, there could be expected reprisals designed to alter our resistance and produce our compliance. Not only was the information itself a product of the programming of our parents by their parents, but also the methods of getting compliance resembled what they had experienced earlier in their own lives.

So, much of the material that became our own belief system **("B")**, was accepted because it was emotionally and physically more economical to do so. This, however, means that within our own developing belief system **("B")** much that we had to accept as **"truth"** might have been:

- Untrue

- Actually damaging

- Inaccurate

- Prejudicial

- Constricting in terms of what we feel we can do

- Limitations on where we can go and what we can do

- One can also see how the transmission of <u>mediocre-to-poor</u> information that is passed from generation to generation:

- Gives rise to ongoing concepts of poor self-worth.

- Builds beliefs and attitudes that are inconsistent with reality.

- Creates and perpetuates prejudice and hatred.

- Robs individuals of a chance to design their own course.

- Limits their courage to break out of the bondage of their <u>current thought.</u>

- Prevents the manifestation of their full potential as human beings.

- Gives rise to mountains of negative feelings toward the perpetrators.

To further illustrate how important it is to understand this dynamic in our thinking,

I urge you to review elements of your own early programming that became the beliefs and unconscious and automatic responses that you use each day.

Observe the various events that occur in your everyday life and note that from your subconscious storehouse of learned responses you are automatically *"knee-jerking"* by responding with conditioned reflex behavior and without giving the issues much conscious thought. It will be helpful to record these observations in a journal so you can review them often. In effect, you are living out your days based on having learned someone else's rules, guidelines and style and, in so doing, you are abdicating your own responsibility for making more effective, meaningful and accountable interactions for maximizing the value of your own life.

- Are any of these programmed concepts preventing you from doing something that you dream of?

- Are any of them generating blocks in your work, and relationships?

- Are you blocked from adventurous exploration of possibilities for your own life?

- Do you habitually and automatically behave in ways that prevent you from being your true self?

The answer has to be a resounding "YES" because we have all been through the same process. Some people had the advantage of higher quality programming; others had devastating programming. In either case, what you learned became the driving force of what you do or don't do today. The truth of this dynamic has been known for years and has generated many adages and aphorisms that for years have told us *"that we become what we think about all day"* that *"what you give your attention to becomes your reality."* They are even more accurate when you realize they consistently tell us that what we hold in our

48

subconscious mind determines our ***"current reality."*** All of it is created by what we were taught to believe is true and workable.

This underscores how crucial it is for us:

- To understand how the mind works.

- To be aware of how we were taught to think about the world.

- To understand that some things we learned have been destructive.

- To assiduously review the contents of our belief system **("B")**.

- To cull out the negative beliefs, assumptions, and expectations that keep us in repetitive behavior that is stifling our emergence to greater futures.

- To insert new self-designed positive beliefs on which to base our enlightened and expanded journey from here on.

- To see ourselves becoming life-long learners who have escaped from the mental prisons that were created by the programming of other people that taught us their ways.

To leave our ***"beliefs"*** unchallenged and unchanged is to close the door to anything different, enlightening and adventurous for our futures.

Our Belief System is:
The stored subconscious memories of all that I have ever experienced:

- My book of *"Rules for the Road"*

- My reference book for all issues—"Have I seen this before?"

- My "modus operandi"—My predictable behavior in given situations.

- My strengths / weaknesses.

- My identity: How others know me. What they expect of me.

- My self-image and my self-worth.

- My habits, attitudes, prejudices and automatic responses.

- My minds filter-i.e. Entrenched programmed thoughts that preclude the entrance of contradictory ideas and keep me locked into old patterns.

- My Ego and its defense mechanisms.

- The Encyclopedic volume of all that I know or think I know!

In our lifetime, this composite set of beliefs, assumptions, expectations and our learned behaviors and habits of thinking will have to address a wide variety of challenges:

Money	Religion
Sex	Love
Hate	Guilt
Work	Responsibility
Emotions	Relationships
Marriage	Childrearing
Recreation	Community
Health	Losses

Dealing with these and other critical life issues can be very difficult under the best of conditions. However, with our programmed and constricted, limited beliefs about our capabilities, about who and what we really are, it becomes a nearly impossible task to handle.

It's time to realize that if we want things to be different for our individual futures, we must change the rogue elements in our *"B"*—the elements that stifle and inhibit our personal growth. We can and must replace those restrictive shackles with upgraded and positive beliefs about ourselves operating in this world. The world itself is one of abundance, great opportunity and excitement that are available when you alter your beliefs and expect and invite these blessings into your personal life. It is with the desiring, the believing, and the opening to new experiences that we can finally leave the circumstances that our present set of beliefs has created for us and move to new, exciting and lofty expressions of our own design for living.

You cannot do it for others and others cannot do it for you. This is a personal decision to no longer simply accept what we were taught. Take the time to review your innermost beliefs and discard those that no longer apply to your adult living. Forego the need to please old programmers by continuing to acquiesce to their pressure. You were designed for more than compliance. You arrived as a newborn with an archetype, a God-given plan for your life. Do not continue to be among those who never discover their potential out of fear of displeasing some other person. It's your life. Uncover your wonderful potential blessings and manifest your life purpose. Each of our lives has been planned by God to be more than simply working, paying bills, staying out of trouble, raising kids and then fading into retirement. If you are not experiencing your bliss, it is nobody's fault but your own. Of course, you were helpless to resist most of the programming in childhood, but, as an adult, it is clearly your prerogative to redesign your existence and "real-ize" (make real) what you are meant to be, do and have.

So, take close looks at some of the beliefs that hamper your current behavior, try to recall the earliest memories of where they came from (who gave you that one) and after the sorting process, choose those that you want to discard and replace them with more wholesome and more realistic beliefs.

Beliefs that <u>aren't true</u> but are held by you to be the "truth" sound like these:

I was their "slow child" and not very smart.

It will never happen for me.

Nothing good will ever happen for me.

I am a screw-up and no good.

I have been a failure from the word go.

I am just like my father and he was no good.

It's too hard.

It's too late.

I am too old.

I tried and it didn't work so I have given up.

I have no right to be successful.

I just can't carry it off. It's too hard.

Life is pitted against me.

None of these <u>have to be true</u>. They are only impression that you gathered in growing up and they were coming from people who felt the same way and taught you their mantras.

They recited them at home for your consumption and you took the bait and swallowed it whole. Given the appropriate mentors who can help you sort and discard such beliefs, you will then be liberated from those thought shackles and able to start anew. It is never too late.

Get on with it!

CHAPTER 8

HOW YOU GOT YOUR BELIEFS

Please go back to the chapter on programming so you can relate the programming lessons that came your way during childhood with the ensuing beliefs that you ended up with.

Most of the programming done with children leans heavily on the fact that we, as parents believe that we have to make things clear to the children, that they are little, troublesome, need constant direction and correction that they can't be trusted to learn a higher echelon of lessons than simply those that say, ***"don't", "you can't", "you mustn't", "don't ever touch my stuff", "you can't talk to me that way",*** and literally hundreds of other prohibitions and warnings that parents use to maintain control. There is also the ubiquitous ***"do it or else"*** that serves as a warning that an infraction of the rules will bring punishment. I can remember hearing the "or else' and recall that on one occasion asking, ***"Let me hear a little bit about the "or else".*** Can the ***"or else"*** be any worse than what we get every day?

Think for a moment that when a child hears repetitive slurs about him/herself, they begin to coalesce into beliefs about his worth, his value, his esteem and those negative beliefs that arise from parental behavior will go into the subconscious as beliefs that wreak havoc for the rest of the individual's life.

Programming	Beliefs that result from programming
Hey, stupid—	I am dumb.
You'll never make it.	A final appraisal of my ability.
You are driving me crazy.	I am in the way and unwelcome.
Speak only when spoken to.	They think I have nothing good to say.
I can't trust you to do anything right.	I am incompetent and a loser.
Stop crying	I have no right to have/show feelings.
Go to your room and stay there.	No one wants me around.
Why can't you be like your sister	I am not alright the way I am.
You're just like your father	Whom I have already learned to hate.
You broke it. You're so clumsy.	I need to restrict myself further.
Get out of my sight.	They can't stand to have me with them.

You get the idea. If most of programming is negative, then beliefs formulated out of the programming material will also be negative, humiliating, shaming and lead the child to withdraw, avoid confrontation and participating in healthy lives. Think back to the programming you received and the beliefs that came out of those early lessons that still persist to this day.

The really pernicious aspect of bad programming is how it tears at the very fabric of the child's soul and once the beliefs are absorbed they are in the unconscious mind forever. Even a competent therapist on the scene later on, cannot easily dislodge the negative that was sown during the early childhood days. I will go on record as saying that it is the incompetence, the ignorance, the thoughtlessness and the callousness of the programming parents and extended family that are flooding the world with psychological and emotional cripples who were once only innocent, wonderful, newborns with great promise and with the inborn potential to be wonderful, effective and fully expressive individuals.

We must find ways to intercept the current practices of raising children and design new approaches to reach and magnify what a newcomer child was designed to be. I am convinced that the negativity of our current practices in our culture is the story behind the deterioration of our very way of life.

Pick up a paper and read about young people in trouble; 40% or more becoming involved in unwed pregnancies, others that rely on dangerous drugs to get through their days, still others who have no idea of appropriate goals for their lives. If you doubt what I am saying, go visit a current high school and see how the already damaged-goods high-schoolers are drifting without aim or direction and are disrupting the classrooms for the others who are serious about getting on with their lives and futures. I understand that the school officials, teachers, principals and educators feel relatively powerless to effect change because they don't have the backing and support of the parents of the kids. So in the school scene we have the "inmates" running the asylum and no one seems able to restore order and effectiveness. Keep it foremost in your mind that these acting out behaviors on the part of young people are stemming from negative influences in their early programming that they were unable to deal with then and have taken on a life of their own in present time and stand as testimony to the influence of their uninformed, ignorant, and indifferent mentors who failed at their tasks of growing healthy kids.

For you adults, recall that this is the generation that will be running the country in a few years. Do you think they have the skills, the intelligence, and the motivation to make our culture a better place in which to live based on their current value systems? They haven't shown consistent abilities and skills to get through their own fundamental educational phase as yet to say nothing about the more complex and tangled issues that will confront them as adults. It is so glaringly obvious that we resemble computers in the aspect that when computers are programmed with inferior soft ware, they cannot produce more sophisticated outputs; it really is "garbage in–garbage out" for us humans also.

It isn't a matter of us not knowing what is necessary to turn it around. But we lack the will, the courage and the determination to regain control over our selves, our children, our environments and our once great position in the world. It will require a really concerted effort to enlist enough support of committed people to turn it around. It isn't rocket science. It is a simple, clear and consistent process that is driven by love, not criticism, support not rejection, commitment not abandonment when the going gets tough. We must find ways to stop the syndrome of "babies" having babies for whom they are woefully unprepared and uncommitted. It is abandoning the process of having surrogate parents (daycare, TV, baby sitters) so the real parents can have two jobs outside the home and ignore the responsibilities of child care. It is not a temporary glitch in the system. It IS <u>THE</u> system that we have allowed to develop and prevail. There is no room for tinkering for a solution. It demands that we find ways back to decent and loving supporting families that will assure the full array of learnings and supporting and loving that will produce restoration of our way of life.

CHAPTER 9

ACTIONS ("A")

Remember we have said that the driving forces behind the actions we take are the beliefs that we hold to be "true". We cannot consistently act or behave differently than our beliefs dictate.

Definition of "Actions": Something done; an act; a deed habitual or usual acts; conduct

Synonyms for Actions ("A")
Decisions
Choices
Behavior
Performance

Have you ever wondered why you go through life doing things in a certain way and it almost seems like it is automatic behavior? Well that's because it **is** virtually automatic because you learned conditioned behaviors when you were little and it is "handy" to let your subconscious mind take over the cues from your beliefs.

Every act that I undertake, of necessity, springs from the contents of my Belief System (**"B"**). It can come from no other place.

I cannot regularly behave in ways other than the ways backed up by what I <u>believe to be true</u>. On occasion, I will do things that I don't believe in but I do so primarily to please someone, surprise someone or defy their expectation.

For me to be "right" there has to be a consistency and integration between what I hold to be true and the actions I take that are driven by my beliefs.

If people ask me to do something that I haven't done before and it is not a part of my experience base, I will have to process it through my **("B")** to see if it is allowable, given what my thoughts tell me.

In part, this is why it is usually unsuccessful for another person to force an action upon us when that behavior clashes with what we have come to believe is "true". "Success" for us comes from doing what we already know how to do and have the permission of our Belief System to proceed with.

This is why diet programs, exercise disciplines, new business ventures, or any other undertakings won't be successful unless and until we hold strong beliefs that it can and will happen for us. If we believe in failure, we will unconsciously act in ways that manifest and validate our belief in failure. The same rule holds if we truly believe in success, we will unconsciously act in ways to cause that success and validate our belief.

Napoleon Hill once wrote:

> *"What the human mind can conceive of and believe in, it can achieve."*

Our beliefs define what we think is possible or impossible for us and nothing beyond that point will happen unless we change the scope and direction of an old belief by replacing it with a new one.

We used to hear the old adage that: **"I'll believe it when I see it."** It seemed to make sense. It was sort of like the Missourian motto: ***"Show me (first) then I will believe it."***

Now it is very clear for many of us that <u>we have to visualize what we want first</u> and only then it can manifest in our life. That could be said thusly: ***I'll see it when I believe it"*** (Belief being necessary before the occurrence).

All of us have the capability of learning to visualize new horizons for ourselves in our mind, going beyond where our current beliefs can reach but we can't do that while clinging tightly to the **"old ways."** The **"old ways"** tend to anchor us in position until we make significant changes. Later on we will talk about how to change those old beliefs by using affirmations as a means of reprogramming your belief system **("B").**

Affirmations are consistently repeated statements about what we want to have happen and believe to be the "truth" in our lives. In fact, all of those parental teachings were our parents' **affirmations** about what they thought they had learned and believed about their own lives and then wanted to instill the same things into our lives, as ***"the way things have to be".*** They repeated those statements to us until we had absorbed their plans for our lives. Their affirmations programmed us in their style. And we have clung to those ***"hand-me-down"*** notions and beliefs as if they were the "truth", valid and unchallengeable.

The time has come belatedly, when we must realize and accept the fact that it is this very same dogged rigidity and refusal to grow out of the negative paradigms of our ancestors and what society dictates that has kept us in shackles and limited living.

We must be willing to take the responsibility for upending the constricted ways and habits of the past and to reach out and invent in our imagination new ways to enter into the experiences of full blown abundant and adventurous living that God designed us to have. It will take a new set of actions on our part but new actions cannot occur until we first address the changing of the belief system components that are the driving force of any actions or choices that we take. It's like removing the **"old way"** to make room for newer and more effective beliefs. Change the beliefs and the actions that follow have to change accordingly. That is the key to growth.

CHAPTER 10

RESULTS ("R")

Definition of "Results": That which proceeds from a set of actions

Synonyms for Results ("R")
Outcomes
Consequences
"Fallout"
Effects (as in "cause and effects")
Occurrences

It is an axiom that our thoughts and beliefs condition our actions and what results from those actions are the consequences that relate to what we have just done. It cannot be otherwise in a world where everything is predicated on "cause and effect" relationships.

This notion is what makes life so predictable once we understand the basic sequential premise—*__thinking / believing / behaving / receiving__.* The patterns of our lives are based on this concept. Our personalities are constructed by the same process. We learn to recognize the rigidity of the beliefs that generate people's behavior and use it to predict what others will do. (We can also use it in planning for desired outcomes because, once we have chosen the goals we wish to reach, we can then develop the necessary action plans to get us to our targets.)

Business planning, military strategies and personal development plans of individuals all capitalize on consciously structuring their activities through a planning procedure to bring desired outcomes. We know that even though goals have been set and action plans carefully laid out, if there is a disruption in the execution of those plans then there will be a predictable change in the consequences. However, remember that midcourse correction of the deviation from plans can restore the direction and the results.

The puzzling factor in the lives of individuals is how many people have missed this lesson in life. They consistently and blindly conduct their everyday lives, doing the same repetitive things that continue to have the same limited outcomes and don't seem to realize that the dysfunctional results they are wallowing in are simply a reenactment of the _**"cause and effect"**_ syndrome. They are oblivious to the fact that what they are "getting" is directly tied to what they are "doing". To receive different outcomes is contingent on changing the aberrant beliefs that distort the actions. When the beliefs are different it is a given that the actions will, of necessity have to change and thus produce different results.

It follows that if you want to have different outcomes in your life, you must "do" something different. The trap is, however, that people have been carefully taught to be fearful, to doubt their own capacities, to limit their expectations and further, that what they are getting is all they can expect. The same mentors who trained them are the ones who would also be on hand to discourage their attempts to do things differently now. Another perverse belief that we hold says that it would be a breach of loyalty to the programmers to do anything that contradicts what they once taught us even if it leads to our failing repeatedly. It's basic. Changing the beliefs then changes the actions and that, in turn, brings different results. Pretty straightforward!

Letting Go

Before you can **get** anything different from this life,

You must first **do** something different.

Before you can **do** anything different with your life,

You must first **know** something different

Before you can **know** anything different,

You must first suspect and then confirm

That it is your present set of **beliefs**

That brings you what you now wish

You could change.

So, in summarizing the formula **"P-BAR"** we have learned:

- Adults programmed us in our infancy and childhood.
- Adults conditioned us to accept their ideas as the **"truth."**
- We learned and stored the lessons in our unconscious mind.
- So we now unconsciously access:
    - ★ A library of warped beliefs and attitudes,
    - ★ Habits of thinking that determine our behavior,
    - ★ Sets of expectations (that our parents taught) for our lives, that are likely giving us poor signals for our own growth.

When confronted by a given event, the subconscious mind will, automatically and without conscious thought, call on those stored lessons and initiate behavior matching what we have been taught is **"right"**. We simply cannot consistently behave in ways that are different than our beliefs. To change our results ("R") we must first change our beliefs that led to those results.

> *"If you always do what you have always done,*
> *You'll always get what you have already gotten."*

Isn't that enough to stimulate you to undertake the changing of the beliefs that are keeping you stagnant?

CHAPTER 11

HALFWAY THERE!

We have now progressed through the **P-BAR** formula about *programming, beliefs, actions and results.* We have looked at those components as a linear, sequential path from infancy to the state of ***"domesticated" adulthood.*** We have learned that the process involves taking a newborn infant with its own innate archetype about life and burying the glory of that archetype beneath an avalanche of collective paradigms that are ***"hand-me-downs"*** from families and society. These programming materials have been lugged down through the ages and passed on to unsuspecting generations of youth who accept them as gospel and try to live lives that make sense out of a mass of dysfunctional and outdated rules.

You can now avail yourself of the incredible opportunity to review your own life against this background for the purpose of discovering the content of your own belief system and understanding how it, moment by moment, dictates the actions that you engage in. When thoughts become beliefs and beliefs drive actions and actions beget outcomes, it is then clear that what you think is what you get. It cannot be otherwise.

Let me emphasize the fact that if you are not happy with what is happening in your life, there is a way to extract yourself from the present state and design a new future based on your own personal choices.

So many psychotherapies and counseling efforts today fail to make this connection. I know because I practiced a number of years as a Psychiatrist, trained to ply our wares in the effort to *"change"* patients. We must forever keep in mind that we cannot effectively change anyone else. We can only change ourselves. The therapist in any relationship cannot force change on the client nor decide what the client's agenda should be. The therapist can only create an open climate in which the client discovers what he/she needs to do and assumes the responsibility for changing him/herself.

It helps to think of the patient in terms of **System Thinking.** Systems are collections of parts that interact in some process. When the parts are in balance with each other, the organism functions effectively. However, when the parts are thrown out of balance for any reason, then the operation of the organism is dysfunctional. It's fair to make an analogy to an automobile. It runs well unless some part of the engine or drive train is out of kilter. Restoring proper operation of the car requires discovering what part is causing the dysfunction and repairing or replacing the part.

Now, consider the state of a **"domesticated"** (socialized) adult human who has been the recipient of years of programming concepts that are rather specific to his family background. He has learned them well, so well, in fact, that their activation is automatic and habitual in the presence of a stimulating event. Another person involved in the same event might have been prepared by an entirely different set of trainers, producing differing viewpoints and outlooks that conflict with the perception of others. How do we then determine who is right or wrong? One or both will engage in behavior and speech designed to win the conflict but it will be settled—less by factual information and more by the strongest set of defensive and coping skills.

Every day each human individual takes his own **"P-BAR"** to work, to social engagements, to all human activities and acts out his/her belief system in those settings. He/she is surrounded by other individuals putting forth their own **"P-BAR"** in efforts to be right, to win, to embarrass or shame others and to come out looking good.

Our organizations, churches, schools, social activities, businesses, recreational activities, family and marital relationships are permeated by negative encounters between the **"P-BARs"** of one participants with that of another participant.

Growing kids are stunted psychologically and emotionally, marriages are sundered, families become dysfunctional, business operations are disrupted and our own general health and welfare are devastated when humans with differing world outlooks get together over differences and conflicts between their individual **"P-BARs"** It is time for a revolution to help people grasp how limited, how imprisoned, how constricted their lives are because our preparation for life is handled in such a cavalier, dysfunctional and thoughtless way by our original programmers.

As pessimistic as some of the foregoing material has seemed, we are at a point where we can be truly optimistic about where we can go from this point. This process of change and growth isn't a free ride. The cost to an individual desiring to bring about effective change includes:

- A burning desire to change.

- Devoting much time and effort in exploring for and identifying those subconscious beliefs that constrict us.

- And a commitment to persevere in the process until lasting changes appears.

Keep foremost in your conscious thoughts that:

Your Thoughts Determine Your Future.

You are the only one that can change your thoughts

Stop waiting for the thought fairy to come along and do it.

What you think each moment leads to a choice of action on your part. It might be a choice of inaction but that is still a form of action.

If you are finding that your life is one in which you feel cramped, crowded and cornered by some circumstances or by beliefs that you have espoused, it is now time to play the role of your own Liberator.

The original journey in growing up looked like this:

$$P \rightarrow B \rightarrow A \rightarrow R$$

Driven by the inputs (**"P"**) from significant adults in your life, you developed your belief system (**"B"**) that became the guiding force for making your choices and decisions (**"A"**). These, in turn, then determined the consequences of those actions and defined your results (**"R"**). You, as an individual had very little to do with the content and quality of what you were given to work with. The (**"R"**) that you are currently experiencing is not the result of good goal setting when you were a child. It is merely the consequences that were produced when you learned to believe as you were taught. We are about to embark on an adventure in which you can redesign your life and create the experiences you were meant to have. Like all good planning processes employed in the business and scientific world, the process should begin at the end (**"R"**) with the careful defining and laying out of what we want to get out of our efforts in the future rather than, as in the first experience in childhood, simply accepting what comes as a result of following dictates from others.

We will be using the same P-BAR formula but we will be reversing the direction this time by starting at the "R" end and working backwards. So let's go on to the next segment, in which we will construct a conscious, purposeful, deliberate definition of exactly what we are looking for in your new "R".

$$P \leftarrow B \leftarrow A \leftarrow R$$

Starting at the **"R"**…at the "end" of the formula we should ask ourselves an important question since we assume that you are not happy with the current **"R"**.

Ask yourself this question and deliberate on the answer. *"What would my new "R" look like if was "fixed" and I had achieved my new goals?* In other words **what goals of my own choosing** would constitute a new exciting **"R"** for a new future for me?

Carefully answer by defining what you would most like the new **"R"** to contain for your gratification. It can be anything you can conceive of, a new house, a new job, car, vacation, additional education, and more income, to complete high school or college education or any other change that would alter your life for the better.

Once you define the new desired goal, then add the detailed aspects of the issue including the minute features. For example, if it is a new car, list the make, the style, the color, and the horsepower so you have an accurate and complete definition of the car you really want, otherwise simply saying you want a different car might just produce an old beater and that won't fit your "goal". You now have defined a working goal that you have chosen, the accomplishment of which would represent a success for you via this process. The more clearly you lay out the details, the closer you will come to realizing your specific goal.

You now have a written goal of your own choosing on which to work. **Label the paper "GOAL"** and for the moment put the paper aside. You aren't ready to work on it yet. Move to the left to the **"Action"** area. The question to ask here is, *"What do I have to do differently than I have been doing, to reach the goal I have set out?"*

Taking another paper now lay out the sequence of steps that will be necessary to activate your goal. The shopping and comparisons of other cars and even the test drives you make will help you make an informed choice so you really get the one you most want.

What is your first step? Determine that you have the money for a new car. Find the showroom for the car you have described. Visit several dealers to decide where you wish to purchase the car. Get an appraisal on your trade-in. Talk to people who have a similar automobile to get their input. Add any other steps that make sense to the task of successfully buying that car.

Now you have an action-plan for the achievement of your goal. You are still not ready to make the purchase. Put this paper aside and label it "**ACTION PLAN**".

Now move to the **Belief area** of the formula. This may be the most difficult work. Begin to explore your belief system to discover what beliefs you have that might get in the way of ultimately buying the car. Such beliefs as *"I shouldn't be* **spending the money right now"** or *"The car I have is good enough to get me around"*, or *"This would be a better car than my parents ever were able to have"They will be upset if I pull this off. I can't do that to them"*!

You are searching for some of those hidden beliefs that you learned and still harbor in your unconscious that would try to discourage you from achieving this goal. Perhaps *a belief that you don't really deserve something this nice*, or *what will people think when I buy something like this?* These are those unconscious gremlin thoughts that have unconsciously held you back from many endeavors in the past. Write down all the beliefs that you feel are obstructions to the goal achievement.

Next, and this might be difficult, but is essential for the process. Try to go back to the days of your programming and recall the actions, the statements, the attitudes of your parents (the programmers). What were their approaches to money, to acquisition of new objects, what did they teach you about deserving or not deserving to have a good life. What did they model for you regarding allowing themselves to have a full life? Were they critical of others that were able to have things? *Did they teach you that you, yourself were not deserving or worthy to have a full life?*

See, we are still on the track of the formula. At this point *we are searching to discover if any of the negative lessons you were programmed with actually did get stored as a "belief" of lack, or inability to reach life fulfillment, or some perceived "wrongness" in wanting more than you have?*

When you begin to make connections between things you learned and how you interpreted their significance for your life, you may able to reevaluate the original lessons that were so negative and the beliefs that you formulated from those experiences and to release the hold that those negative beliefs have on the ways you think you have to live.

It should be stated here and emphatically—Most of the programming we all got was negative. Repeated during our growing up, the *junk lessons became junk beliefs that told us we were wrong, dumb, stupid, lazy, undeserving and would never make it in the real world. We were told not to get our hopes up because we would only be disappointed if it doesn't work out.* So we learned to settle for mediocrity and avoided any serious dreaming of better lives to come.

If you are starting to think that this kind of programming only happened in your own family, let me emphasize that by far the majority of people who are alive today had similar or even worse experiences in trying to survive infancy and childhood and to grow up to enter the adult world effectively.

The chaos, the violence, the abuses, the failures, the broken relationships, the depressions and suicides in today's world all had their start in the early days of childhood and family life and in the totally inadequate and negative processes that get labeled as childrearing. It is an unrelenting and unavoidable responsibility for all of us to undertake the task of *changing what we all do to each other in the process of daily living.* You can help the process by taking yourself through the process of undoing all the crap that happened to you—which you have dragged along until now.

All of the disordered thinking, the pathological ways in which we carry on daily life, the wretched things we do to each other our of fear and vengeance came originally from nothing more than negative thoughts of sick and unhappy people who told us that their way was the only way to live life. They were so very wrong and their wrongness carried over to your beliefs about yourself that must be trashed because you are a full fledged child of God who intended for you to savor the best of everything on this planet.

Try to make joy and happiness and productive living out of that mess that you were taught and it will never happen until we agree to stop our own participation in the ugliness. We can't stop others directly but it has to begin with someone so why not you and me?

I have read and heard discussions about how many people it would take to bring lasting and global change. I thought it would be in the millions to get the job done. But scientists and people who work numbers say that 100,000 truly dedicated people could make it happen. I am trying to be one of those. Would you like to join with me?

In subsequent chapters I have suggested that there are some relatively simple changes in thinking that would help the process. I started out just like the rest of you. I have had to do a lot of remake in my life, am still not at the end of the process but I am a lot different than I used to be and it goes better that way.

I have a chapter on *"Things That I Had to Learn"*, a chapter on some of the common human behaviors that contribute to the chaos, and chapters on how we might begin to modify what we do, setting the example for others to follow. I hope you read on.

CHAPTER 12

THINGS I NEEDED TO LEARN

(And things I needed to unlearn)

Very few people escape the drudgery and pain of having to learn lessons that don't make sense just because their parents said so. When we are little and relatively powerless, it is impossible to challenge the words of parents and extended family or later the teachers or other authorities that enter our lives.

I was no exception. I grew up in a single parent home in the 20's and 30's when things were even more stringent than they are today. I was fatherless at the age of three and my mother never remarried and there were no siblings to compare notes with.

Further, my mother was a grade school teacher that further qualified her as an authority about what kids need to know. I had my mother for a fifth grade teacher which only exacerbated the emphasis she placed on seeing that I received the "right" lessons.

She was hypochondrical and rather constantly concerned with her real and imagined illnesses and she used them to control my behavior by reminding me (while clutching her chest) that I would certainly be the death of her when I was simply trying to be a kid, and a good one at that.

I remember one of her teachings always began with, **"*Bobby, don't do that (or say that, or act like that, or look like that,) what would peo-***

ple think? It was a common preamble to the criticism that followed her describing my alleged misdemeanor. After a number of repetitions of a phrase like that, one becomes concerned, really concerned about *"what do people think"*. I think I finally broke out of that trap when I was about 35 years old and begin to not care what *"those people were thinking about me."*

Another one went something like this: *"That elderly couple have neither chick nor child so be nice to them and they might leave you something"*. As it turned out, I wasted a lot of "nice" with no results to show for it but it was a totally inappropriate lesson to be foisted on a child under any conditions.

There were immutable rules about how I should eat, how to stop slouching, that bedtime was 7:30pm, do your chores, don't talk back to me, your mother, respect your elders, no matter what they were like, stop complaining that the argyle socks and the cable type sweaters she was forever knitting for me that were always loose and over-sized really made me look strange going to school. I often wondered then if I looked as good as she said I did, in loose knitting, why did the other kids laugh as I passed by?

These were only a few of the annoyances that came wrapped as lessons about how to be. I know that you, dear reader, had your own set of things learned in your home that didn't mesh with your own feelings. But that was then and this is now and it's all water over the dam. In recalling the other good things my mother did for me, these were rather insignificant but nonetheless, it is vital that parents begin to realize that the children do have feelings and emotions that need careful tending to avoid shame and humiliation issues.

What follows here is a listing of the things that I have had to re-consider and change while I was growing up and trying to sort out the *"junk"*. Perhaps it will encourage you to modify or scrap a few of your own beliefs.

P-BAR REVISITED

Here are a few examples of things I had to change.

Life isn't always fair.

What we are taught doesn't always work.

Some of what we're taught has been wrong forever and it still gets passed on—parents to kids, elders to newcomers, because we're caught up in, stuck in, attached to, and trapped into rituals, lies and dysfunctional behavior called *"raising kids"*.

A lot of what we do to our kids echoes what was done to us in the name of childrearing, socializing kids, life-preparation, training etc.

How to fight fair. How to be open to hear the other side. How to not let the importance of always "being right" determine the tactics I use against another person.

How to share.

How some people will screw you every chance they get. It's just the way they are. Stop waiting for them to change. Find new people to work, play, and learn from.

Nothing is 50-50. Everyone involved should be giving 100% to the effort.

How doing *"good"* isn't always rewarded but do your good anyway.

Why sometimes anger is all right.

How we were taught to believe that we were born in sin. Wrong! We were born in innocence and all of the troubles we continue to encounter are derived from the distortions, lies and mis-information that we were taught in the process of our families and mentors "socializing" us to match societal standards.

How grown-ups aren't always wiser but you have to pretend they are just to get along at times.

Father/mother/teacher/doctor/lawyer, and Indian chief aren't always good and right, honest or loving; don't always know best.

How sometimes those who are most demanding of us are the best mentors for our ultimate outcomes.

All about manipulation, guilt, shame, humiliation and how some people use them to intimidate and control others.

How less than the whole truth isn't bad—occasionally.

How rainy days aren't all bad.

That too many sunny days aren't always good.

That retreat isn't always cowardice.

That attack is sometimes necessary.

That the best of efforts at times don't get it done.

That nothing matters as much as we think it does.

That sometimes our fondest desires wouldn't be good for us in the long run.

That people lie, deceive, cheat and distort a lot—to get their own way.

That things taught in the name of religion are not always true.

That "religious" and "spiritual" don't mean the same thing.

That we have many "idols" that we "worship" that take us in wrong directions.

That smiles are sometimes dangerous cover-ups.

That people make a lot of excuses for being *"wrong"*.

"Secondary gain" is an important concept to understand. It often helps to understand people and situations to explore what possible advantages might be inherent and hidden in the behaviors of people that don't make seem to be obvious on the surface.

"Secondary gain" refers to the situation where a person appears to remain in an unpleasant space that we can't understand on the surface but the individual sees him/herself benefiting from being there. The *"secondary gain"* is the advantage the person perceives that wouldn't happen otherwise like clinging to feigned illness because it results in getting out of work, responsibilities or other activities that are unwanted.

Most people that end up being selfish, thoughtless, and inconsiderate do so because they have focused on and practiced being self-centered.

The main purpose of using anger toward others is to intimidate the others into changing their behavior to coincide with the way *we want* them to be.

Anytime anyone uses anger with us they want us to give in to them, give up our position and cave.

Giving in to the angry manipulation of others doesn't bring peace because it leaves behind resentment—the seeds of future retaliation.

That often avoiding confrontation leaves the issue unresolved for another go around later.

That *"pleasing others"* never ends once you start.

That *"rescuing"* people who don't want to be your target (your defined victim) doesn't bring you their gratitude.

That when someone describes to you their current situation, sometimes they don't want your solution or advice, but only to have someone <u>listen to them.</u>

That what is true today might not be the same truth in the future.

That *"love"* doesn't always land correctly.

That ***"making love"*** is often a misnomer if it is done with the mindset of making a conquest.

That ***"making love"*** is often nothing more than someone else's need to use another person.

That someone's ***"giving in"*** isn't always what you think it is.

That dawn always follows the darkest night.

That sometimes our fears <u>invent</u> impregnable monsters that we can't seem to vanquish.

That nothing is ever as bad as our fears make it.

That not letting yesterday die with the nighttime keeps us chained to our pasts that were designed by others.

That most issues we try to settle (win) don't get resolved by logic alone.

That the 10 Commandments aren't bad for starters.

That not everyone else will necessarily be as committed to the 10 Commandments as you might be.

That returning negative for negative is stupid.

Never coddle a mal-content.

That giving in to threats never brings peace; but only makes you appear more susceptible to continuing threats.

That guile is transparent. Learn to recognize and see through it.

That often things aren't what they seem to be and you might just be right about it.

That most of what we continually go to the wall for isn't really worth it.

That meditation and self-exploration, well done, leads to true freedom.

Giving in to keep peace seldom succeeds. Your sense of losing and being 'had' will see to that.

The "best" families, neighborhoods, schools, churches, clubs—aren't always.

That if you spend serious time learning about human nature, about control, manipulation, "being used", how we employ put downs, etc you will fare better in life.

Superiority is mostly a figment of imagination by the "owner", contrived as a behavior or a costume to conceal gross inferiority and inadequacy.

At the core bullies are massive cowards and their outward behavior is a sham.

If it feels insincere coming at you, it probably is.

If you want to see peace, innocence and perfection, gaze at a newborn.

A person with many excuses is a person who needs them. Don't invest heavily in the relationship.

Loud voices are fear seeking to appear impregnable.

Everything your eyes fall upon is God in manifestation.

Storms, as bad as they can be, pass.

Being unconditional in your loving takes great courage and strength.

Being unconditional with your loving won't always get you high marks but it will lead you to a great character and peace.

Church isn't always a sacred place. Great selfishness, greed, dysfunctional behavior masquerade as piety.

Being judgmental of others is often a projection of our own perceived negative self-worth onto others.

We tend to dislike people and behaviors that are reflections of ourselves.

You can't alter another's behavior by attacking the behavior. The behavior always arises from some core belief that must first be changed. Then with a new belief there is a path for new behavior to follow.

90% of our early life programming (lessons, rules, and prohibitions) was negative in flavor. (What would 90 % of positive programming have looked like and how might we have turned out differently?)

We care more about what people think of us and our behavior than we care about what we become by doing it.

How did the opinions of others come to be so important to us?

In early life it's the opinions of our parents and close people around us that we think is a true measure of us. Think about that one for a while.

You were perfect when you arrived. Who were the ones that tampered with that perfection by instilling their own standards and opinions into your belief system?

Here's a big one. You have as much right to be "you" without interference as "they" do. Take action to be yourself.

Sometimes bad people seem to get all the "good" things but—

1. Eternity isn't over

2. What have you defined as desirable *"good"* things?

3. How much would you give up of yourself to have one of them?

Maybe what you had your heart set on—isn't so wonderful.

A rainbow seen in its purity can erase a lot of negative stuff, if you'll let it.

"Stuff" is only that—*"stuff"*! Look at it again with different eyes.

In the end—what you become shouldn't represent what others wanted you to be but what the Universe intended for you to become.

Life is about you being you regardless of the opinions of others.

Step forth in your own being and rejoice.

You probably have some of your own thoughts to add to this list. Go ahead and get them out where you can really see them. They are only your thoughts and you have a right to alter them anyway you see fit.

CHAPTER 13

THINGS WE ALL NEED TO KNOW

The world in which we live is a complex organism and negotiating our way from infancy to mature and successful adult life requires that we know a lot about how to make things happen in the way we want them to be.

We need to understand how to live in this world safely, effectively, happily, in relationships that matter and that work. We need to know how to extract joy and love and peace that this Universe has the potential to bring forth.

Ask yourself the question, "What would a person need to experience and learn from infancy through adolescence to the adult state, in order to maximize the quality of life that he/she desires?"

The very first issues have to do with just the handling of the physical self so there is physical safety for him/her. In the beginning he/she needs a lot of adult buffering just to avoid the commonplace injuries and compromises that will occur. He/she needs to have the proper nutrition, cleansing, dressing, housing and protective care that assures basic life support needs.

There is an ongoing need for loving attention, closeness to the caregivers and a sense of "belonging to" and being wanted by other members of the familial structure.

He/she needs caregivers that intuit the diverse needs to be comforted, to be cherished, to be accepted and to be shielded from frightening and threatening experiences that can topple the individual's sense of personal security.

For optimal living we all need to know that basic functions and needs will be present for us as we progress through our maturation to adulthood.

We need to learn how to avoid the ubiquitous assaults from others in the form of:

Fear	Criticism
Hurt	Injury
Degradation	Rejection
Torment	Separation
Abuse	Humiliation
Physical attack	Shaming

All of these negative encounters have the potential to hamper, even prevent us from attaining our full human capacity. Our lives are constantly bombarded by people using these various ploys to gain control over us, to keep us from reaching our target goals so that we appear to be "less than they feel they are" and thus we fall into victimhood that stays with us. We must learn how to sidestep all of these kinds of manipulations in order to be open to what the Universe is holding out for us.

We also need to prevent ourselves from learning and adopting these same destructive behaviors toward others that we encounter in daily living.

We need to learn that the world is full of people who go about creating their own set of victims so they can justify taking the role of "rescuer" and thereby feeling superior to those they have put into dependent positions.

You need to understand why some people are "perfectionists" and "pleasers" and the reasons why they have been willing to take on those roles. It all has to do with trying to elicit respect, love and acceptance from manipulative people who feel entitled to set the parameters for "what should be" and to reject those that "fail" to meet their expectations.

We need to recognize the profound separation that we feel from one another and how it came into being because of our own selfishness, our own manipulation of others and the obvious maneuvers we use to push people away in order to feel safer.

We need to know that each of us is a living, breathing, and valuable child of God and as such we are entitled to the best of what the Universe can offer.

We need to understand that no one has the right to prevent our full citizenship in the world nor do we have the right to deny it to others.

We need to know that the Creator (God) has provided a luxurious world in which we can all enjoy the wonders of nature, that all of our needs have been provided for, that they are there for sharing not hoarding, and that there is enough to go around to all people.

We need to know that we share the responsibility toward one another to be fair, loving, and cooperative, in all transactions that involve us.

We need to understand that our own selfishness, our greed, our envy, our anger, our attacks and our depreciation of anyone else eventually leads to counter measures that introduce conflict, hatred, jealousy and place all of us in jeopardy and risk.

We need to know that in our lifetime, we have a better than even chance that we will be in a relationship with someone who proves to be less than we thought and is a source of conflict and disruption of our lives. If we have gone though the process of trying to resolve the situation and there is no evidence of improvement, we need to know that it is often necessary to break away from the toxic relationship and start off in a new direction that is more productive. Too many people remain in horrific situations thinking they can never get out of the mess and they stay and waste more life energy than it is worth.

We need to remind ourselves constantly that we are all children of God and that as such we are loved unconditionally by Him and He can put our lives back together as they were intended to be.

We need to be constantly conscious of the presence of toxic people who like nothing better than making the lives of others miserable. These people need to be denied entrance to our life spaces, to be kept out of range of our environment and not allowed to encroach within the boundaries that we have established.

When you attempt to erect those boundaries that define your space, there will be people who are upset with you and will challenge you by trying to violate your space. It is not only your prerogative but also an essential responsibility to yourself to uphold and defend the boundaries that spell your peace and safety regardless of people's relationship to you.

All of the above issues can appear to be overwhelming and difficult to make happen but once you decide how you want your piece of life to look, taste and feel, you will find ways to design desirable outcomes that will last.

Lastly and most importantly, you need to know beyond a doubt that there is a loving, non-judgmental God, Creator that lives within your cell structure and constantly monitors and guides your search for union with Him. He will never force, never punish, never reject your efforts since He has given us all "Free Will", but through subtle messages and urgings you will know that His hand is on your life if you will just let go of our preconceptions.

CHAPTER 14

EGOS AT WORK

"EGO" is Latin for "I".

Considering the **EGO** that each of us develops from birth and over time, its function is to provide us with an interface for dealing with the world, its people and all of the challenges that come our way.

Recognize that **EGO** is not present at the time of birth but the infrastructure for its ultimate development exists in the neurological structure of the cognitive brain. This nascent **EGO structure** receives all of the sensory inputs from the child's early environment that fall under the label of early life "programming" where we are taught what society and parents think we should know. What a shame that parents and other trainers don't realize the incredible power they exercise in laying down the teachings and foundations for the life of their child that is unfolding and yet, in the process of raising the child they often ignore the incredible impact that their influence has in preparing the young mind with lessons that are often inaccurate, lies, and distortions of the truth. In addition, the examples and modeling behavior that we observe in relation to our parents is often a sub-optimal basis for us to copy and carry with us through life.

The "**EGO**", the "I" of our makeup is a collection of learned responses that develop over the span of our lifetime. Most of it is a derivation from the early life programming that we receive from parents and other mentors. Others refer to this collection as our ***"belief system"*** or our ***"life style"*** or our ***"personality"*** and it includes all of our:

- Beliefs

- Expectations

- Assumptions

- Attitudes

- Fears

- Dreams

- Habits

- Family and societal myths

- Prejudices

- Filters

- Rules and prohibitions

- The estimates by others that we accepted about our abilities etc.

- Coping mechanisms **("EGO Defense mechanisms")**

  - ★ Repression

  - ★ Suppression

  - ★ Denial

  - ★ Projection

  - ★ Displacement

  - ★ Reaction Formation

By the age of 10 years, major parts of the **EGO** have been assimilated by the child and the remaining years of adolescence embellish and

imbed these ideas indelibly into the neurological structure of the individual. In theory then, the adolescent or young adult is prepared to
go forth and meet the world. This would be a wonderfully exciting
period for the young individual **IF**, the lessons, the beliefs, the habits,
the dreams and the modeling that are taught were of the highest cali-
ber, truthful and devoid of flaws.

Such is most often not the case, however. The concepts and beliefs that are imparted to the child during their early life preparation
are and can only be as good as the beliefs, prejudices, lessons, fears,
lies, and misinformed thoughts that the parents harbor as their own
"truth". No one can teach what he or she doesn't know.

So because of the widely diverse, distorted, often untrue, and misinformed information that is placed in the heads of our young by their
elders, we continue to perpetuate the same defects, the same lies, the
same corrosive beliefs, the same dysfunctional paradigms that keep
our fractured lives and crippled culture struggling.

The humiliation, the fears, the abuses, the lack of love and forgiveness, the gross misinformation that is imparted and the flawed parental
modeling examples provided in the process of raising our precious
children guarantees that they will have nothing more noble, more
loving, more effective to give to their offspring than what they have
received in their own programming period.

Mediocrity results if we are lucky; less fortunately it contributes
to the steady and slowly deteriorating quality of overall human relationships that breeds the violence, the dishonesty, the disruptive patterns, and the totally destructive confrontations that are so prevalent
today.

Consider the fact that each of us is driven by our own **"EGO"** or
"belief system" that gives rise to our daily actions and subsequently
determines our outcomes and experiences. If the learned contents of
our **"EGO"** contain faulty information and flawed opinions of our
parents and mentors and distorted paradigms about life and its processes, then our subsequent actions and behaviors stemming from such
limited learnings must also be limited and incomplete.

Consider that our "EGOs" have the task of:

- Giving definition and direction to our lives.

- Protecting us from the assaults of the "**EGOs**" of other people.

- Helping us to manifest the best possible imagery of ourselves.

- Reducing the competition and threat from others.

- Covering up the internally recognized shortcomings that we harbor about ourselves.

- Trying to make sense out of our daily struggles and confrontations.

- Maintaining our status quo for consistency.

- Keeping us "safe" by maintaining our "sameness".

- Furthermore, our **EGOs** are very busy doing other things for us:

- **EGO** organizes and directs our daily behaviors to be consistent with our belief system.

- **EGO** projects thoughts into the future based upon our past experience.

- (Thus experiences in a future time resemble what we have already seen before—maintaining our status quo).

- **EGO** pretends, negotiates, blusters and aspires.

- It provides all these services as a method of protecting, preserving and cultivating our personality.

- It sees the ideas, actions and encounters with other people as potentially threatening and activates the EGO defenses to minimize the threat to self.

To accomplish these outcomes we are relying almost totally on a collection of assimilated teachings from people who have already been involved in their own, often-unsuccessful life-long struggles with doubts, fears, unfulfilled dreams and shattered hopes. It's no wonder that our current reality is defined by disruption and dysfunction, by trauma from street conflict to global wars, from poverty and want to fractured homes and families. Visualize these individual collections of thoughts and beliefs in daily, even hour-by-hour conflict in the service of helping each of us come out on top of all the others.

No wonder that in our extreme levels of frustration, we are destroying each other and the planet on which we live. The selfishness that is implied in these confrontations and manipulations is of immense proportions and completely precludes the expressions of love, compassion and collaboration that we are so lacking yet otherwise potentially capable of.

It is sad to realize that the contents of our current belief systems represents little if any original thought but rather is mostly the collections of parental and societal belief systems that were transferred to us in a climate of "do it—or else ". We accepted these hand-me-down operating instructions in an aura of fear not love and, unfortunately have probably done the same thing to our own offspring.

It would be interesting if you took a bit of time to consider what your life would be like today if, instead of being raised in your own home of origin, you had been raised by another family three blocks down the street. How would your approach to life be different today? What different beliefs, hopes, expectations, prejudices and experiences would you possess if your heads had been filled with different rules, prohibitions, attitudes, habits, and beliefs? You see, we are really only vehicles for the perpetuation of the current societal practices through the process of being taught the acceptable lessons and ways of the culture and being expected to learn and practice such ways until we can pass it on intact to the next generation.

It is "society's relay race" in which the knowledge base of our ancestors is the baton that is passed on from great grandparents to grandparents, grandparents to parents and then to us for an ultimate handoff to our own kids. It's meant to be a way of preserving the current culture for our progeny and, unfortunately it does just that. As long as that paradigm of hand-me-down teaching is in place there is little hope for changing the patterns and instilling new and more effective ways of experiencing life.

Each of the major religions tells us that we are special at birth, that we arrive imbued by the universal energy that is GOD. They also tell us that the qualities of being non-judgmental and expressing unconditional love toward one another are dependable ways to change our world. They tell us that love conquers all. Momentarily we pause and tell ourselves that would be better than what we are experiencing but then we return to the old format because it is familiar, requires no new learning, no effort to change and we rejoin the masses that are caught up in societal and planetary chaos.

In many ways they also tell us that living from the orientation of our human **EGOs** creates the selfishness and conflict that we experience. Furthermore, they all talk about the need to get rid of attachments to our negative paradigms in order to be free of guilt, shame, limited capabilities and dysfunction (the very things we were so carefully taught). But when we try to make such changes, we are subject to the derision and rejection of the people who are caught up in the fostering and perpetuation of the same old ways.

The inscribed teachings of our mentors have been so strong and the negative consequences we expect when we deviate from their admonitions are so dire that we choose to cling to crippling concepts rather than launch out for the paradise that God intended us to experience.

The Ego lessons derived from our early training includes:

- Always needing to be "right".

- Winning at any cost.

- Being quiet, clean and orderly to please adults.

- Basing our actions on what people will think?

- Being a pleaser.

- Avoiding confrontation to "keep friends".

- Not revealing "family secrets."

- Protecting the family members regardless of circumstances.

- Avoiding acceptance of responsibility or fault.

- Religion.

- Money.

- Sex.

- Manners.

- Integrity, honesty, ethics, interpersonal relationships.

- Work ethic.

- Patriotism and political issues.

- Marriage and family.

- Death and dying.

Think on what our **EGO** is all about; how it is riddled with beliefs that are the driving force behind the actions we take all day. Think about how every other human we encounter also has an **Ego** that was put together in the same way as ours, out of the distorted and flawed lessons of their parents and their segment of society, and you get a solid glimpse of why there is violence, greed, selfishness, separation, attack, character assassination, envy, jealousy and pathological maneuvers to neutralize other people whom we have designated as our "enemies".

These confrontations that we all deal with day to day can't really be resolved by reason, by arbitration, by becoming the "alpha dog" in our lives, or simply one person deciding to give in to the aggressor, (there are too many examples of what subjugation does to the human psyche). There is only one way to ultimately resolve these countless mini–wars going on each day and that is by realizing that only love for one another, seeing ourselves in each other, realizing that however it has seemed and been handed down the centuries, it isn't working and further progression of our conflicted selves is destroying the planet and all of us with it.

It also explains why, over the centuries, the major religions-Kabbalah, Buddhism, Hinduism and Christianity have all admonished us to get rid of our divisive behaviors (our EGO's), to embrace universal love as a unifying power and realize and accept our common cosmic heritage that could usher in a new planetary wholeness.

In the next chapter, I have included the most common "tools" of Egos in the attempts to manipulate and control those around us. We all use these "defenses mechanisms" and we all need to stop our daily annihilation of fellow travelers on the road in search of peace and mutual acceptance of our common humanness.

CHAPTER 15

EGO DEFENSES

Definition: An **"ego defense mechanism"** is an <u>unconscious,</u>(we aren't aware we are using them) learned behavior intended to protect us and to control the impact of harmful actions from others as well as to disguise the motivations and intents of what we do to other people

<u>They are mechanisms to:</u>

- Hide painful, shameful thoughts or events from the conscious awareness of others and ourselves.

- Avoid responsibility, accountability and punishment

- Shift blame to others and disown our involvement.

- Enhance one's self-image related to that of others.

- Justify holding negative feelings toward others believed to have done wrong.

Basic Ego Defense Mechanisms:

Suppression   Introjection
Repression   Reaction Formation
Denial   Displacement
Projection   Dissociation

These defense mechanisms are ways of behaving that are designed to obfuscate the intentions of the aggressive and controlling actions that we encounter in everyday living. We weren't born knowing them but as we faced and dealt with the issues and people that constituted our early life experiences, we picked these lessons up, learned them, stored them in our unconscious mind and use them to control the impact of unwanted emotional feelings that accompany the fears and hurts that came our way. I think it is important for you to understand them. They are behaviors that we all use to control what is happening around us (and recall that others are using them in relationship to us.) Bear in mind that we are generally unaware that we are using these devices because they arise from our unconscious mind.

Suppression:

The semiconscious process of curbing and containing our behavior to avoid being "found out". We are generally aware that we are attempting to keep some issue under wraps and at least partially secreted from the events of the present moment.

Repression:

The unconscious action to stuff the unwanted information in our thoughts into our unconscious to hide it from view and recognition by others and ourselves. It is cramming down or "bottling up" feelings and behavior that we don't want to be responsible for.

Denial:

Usually preceded by repression, denial is our professing that the unwanted material is not true and doesn't exist. This is added to reinforce the hiding of undesirable behavior.

Projection:

Projection is our disowning what is unpleasant or undesirable and mechanism is prominent in paranoia.

Reaction Formation:

This is the unconscious process of acting outwardly the opposite of how we feel inwardly. If we are frightened and feeling inadequate inside, it is behaving in opposite fashion externally to conceal our terror or anger that is held inside. For a person who is a raging cauldron of anger internally, reaction formation is an attempt to convince others and him or herself that he/she is not a threat. His/her external behavior takes on the appearance of over-politeness and obsequious behavior. In the case of the overly polite individual, beware that there is much negative energy waiting for expression and the individual is fearful. The same thought applies to the bully. He is also concealing his internal feelings but in this case the feelings are those of inadequacy, weakness and vulnerability. Remembering this, you gain power over the bully knowing that he is acting to hide his significant fears. He believes that by appearing to be menacing externally, he will create a zone around him in which he can feel safer and more isolated from those he thinks constitute a threat to him.

Displacement:

It is the unconscious transfer of negative thoughts and emotions that arose in the workplace where it is handed off to the secretary or other person not in a position to react. Or anger generated at work toward the boss that can't be expressed because of possible consequences but it can be displaced to the wife, children or the dog later.

In addition to the "Ego defense mechanisms", there are other learned behaviors and mannerisms that we all learn to use to control our environment and the people in it.

Withdrawal

Pouting

Crying

Avoiding

Eye-rolling, grimacing

Smirking

Ignoring

Labeling name-calling

Avoiding eye contact

Withholding

Anger

Space invasion

Prejudice

Stereotyping

Overreacting (either way)

Judging

Shifting attention away from.

Assigning roles to others they haven't agreed to accept

We have all used these singly or in combination with other behaviors and we do it without being consciously aware that we are trying to control and manipulate situations that arise. Others are also using these same ploys against you in encounters with them. It is when the manipulations and controlling behaviors of people or groups collide that we generate the pathological relationships that we struggle with every day. Each side is trying to make the opponents back off, give in or otherwise be neutralized.

Looking at the nature of and implications that arise from the various defense mechanisms of the EGO, it becomes apparent that most of those efforts are of a negative nature and are designed to be constrictive rather than expansive. They were learned and adopted during our growing up from infancy to adulthood to make our immediate surroundings seem safer, to protect us from criticism, abuse and attack from those who are bigger, more powerful and have greater capacity to hurt us.

Each of these mechanisms is a learned way to keep troublesome thoughts and behavior out of the present scene because we have found the expression of such things to be challenging to those who control us. Look again at the purpose of each defense and you will see that the design is to hide or conceal that what we have been taught is dangerous, unappealing or unwelcome negative thoughts or behaviors. If we can successfully prevent them from surfacing in our interactions with bigger more powerful people, we will be safer than if we lose control of them and they come tumbling out.

The net effect is that our defenses, although they protect us and hide what we don't want exposed, they do limit what we can do in a whole variety of life experiences. The protection thing is good if we live in a precarious or dysfunctional family. The limitation thing is bad because it prevents us from learning a full repertoire of human experiences that can illuminate our lives and bring a sense of fulfillment and satisfaction.

It is crucial to see and realize that the development of these various behavioral mechanisms has its genesis in the earliest parts of our lives. We aren't born with these skills. They only come about through our attempts to control our environment and limit our exposure to noxious experiences. It should also be appreciated that every home and family will have its own style based on the beliefs, assumptions, and habits of the people who live there. So, if you know what your own basic defenses are and how you behave to maximize your acceptance by others in the place where you now live, realize that the others in that same home have their favorite ways of interacting and manipulating and these different ways of doing things often clash.

Further research will demonstrate the numerous similarities between your own nuclear family performance and the two families that gave rise to your parents (your maternal and paternal grandparents) and their set of behaviors, beliefs and habits. Much of the programming content that has become our set of rules, prohibitions, restraints, was nothing more than hand-me-down yardsticks about how to act and "be" in the world.

If you have already accepted the programming that you received in growing up without much resistance, you are probably laboring under many limiting and constricting conventions that are shaping and defining what you are able to dream of and accomplish. You may even be among those who really believe that they have already reached the apex of life that was possible for them. They believe that they cannot expect to go and grow further. "Be satisfied with what you have—you'll only be disappointed if you want more". Nothing could be farther from the truth. Even though you may have been hobbled by the rules of childhood, it is possible, even desirable that you study the content of PBAR and realize it can be a liberating force as you realize you have a God-given right to be all you can be and if that disturbs someone in your family or a set of your acquaintants, walk away from their influence and their manipulations and rise to your full potential.

Over the centuries, billions of human lives have been wasted because of such beliefs and conditioning. We continue to do the same thing today even in this world of scientific breakthroughs. Little time and effort is devoted to exploring the depths of the human mind and soul to see what our potentials are and what life would look like if we were released from this bondage.

I found that when I became aware that I was using these defenses and looking as dysfunctional as some of these actions suggest, I wanted to begin to eradicate them from my repertoire and take on more adult and appropriate behavioral patterns. You need to start consciously observing where and how you can develop more effective ways to change your negative beliefs about yourself to a new set of positive affirmations about your right to shed the old paradigms that were given to you in childhood and to adopt a fuller way of life.

CHAPTER 16

IT'S NOT HARD TO UNDERSTAND

All of the preceding words are simply an explanation of how we got to be where we are now.

There is nothing mysterious about how we develop as individuals. Everything we now know started simply as something that others taught us to repeat over and over until our brain got the message and we couldn't forget it. After a dozen or two repetitions, the concept becomes no longer simply words but takes on the character of being a "truth" or a "belief". That's how we did it with the alphabet, with multiplication of numbers, of acquiring a baseline of information about things that we were going to need to live successfully.

The only thing that makes a profound difference is the inherent accuracy and real truth of what we are being taught. Whatever we hear in our homes that is touted to be important will, when repeated enough times become an indelible "fact" for life in that particular home. I say that because, you might learn things that characterize your particular home and resonate with the other inhabitants but if you take those lessons to a home in which they are not honored and different concepts are promulgated, big misunderstandings will arise and cause disruption of equanimity. Those ideas and concept will not fly in homes where they are not regarded as the "way it is".

Have you ever wondered what your life would be like today, how different from your current situation if, as a newborn instead of going to the home in which you grew up, you were raised in a home three blocks down the street? Or even more strangely if you had been given to a family in a completely different culture, with a different language and customs? Your whole education would have been different (and naturally so).

Or if you had had the experience of confused and addled parents who taught you that the piano was really called a bed, a chair was called a book, and other items were misnamed. You would have been expected to learn what prevailed in that home and you would have done so, but what chaos when you left the home, entered the world outside that home and tried to carry on a conversation with other people.

It's no different than if the home of origin for you, taught you that love was weakness, that anger was a virtue, that assaulting people was a means of getting your own way, that tenderness and consideration for others was a blatant sign of stupidity. Many homes resemble such a place, perhaps more by what they model than what they teach, but nonetheless, the incorrectness of what you would learn in that home would render you a misfit in the world where you have to live, work and hangout. Today we are faced with the fact that nearly 60% of marriages terminate in divorce, 40% of all children born are to a single parent with no visible means of support and certainly not prepared to optimize the development of the child. Those percentages guarantee failure for the children to thrive, and often failure to even survive. Can you see the central importance of coming to our senses, showing, documenting and changing the way in which we allow so many children to grow up in impoverished, pathological and toxic homes?

The overwhelming numbers of people who are not prepared properly for adult life, the numbers of children who are robbed of their birthright to decent upbringing, the huge numbers of psychologically crippled people as a result of improper early life care attest to our failure as a society to define and alter the most basic of living and learning experiences for our population.

And it is not only the homes that are failing our young. Our schools, even our churches have lost their influence and the media, particularly TV have heavily contributed to the decline of quality of life experiences that model value lessons for all of us to absorb and to practice.

Here I took a break from putting words on the page and took time to decide whether I was overboard on the things I am laying out. I am convinced that things really are as bad as I am portraying them. I consider all of what has been laid out before you on these pages is a fair treatment of my concern. The issue is what are we, collectively going to do to cause change? It can't become anything different by turning our backs, or by stating that it is too far gone to address. I believe that any of us who still have years left in our life, should be stirred to action and become committed to participating in efforts to turn things around. If you don't see it as that important, then perhaps you are part of the ongoing problem.

Consider the size and heaviness of what is going wrong and if you agree, talk to others you know, enlist them to explore ways with you to do something about our common plight. You know groups of people, you belong to clusters of people either at work or church or neighborhood who are part of the scene. All of you and more are needed to tackle the chore. It's not really bigger than we are. It is simply more relentless than we are. If enough people agree that it is worthy of remedy, we can find a way together.

CHAPTER 17

HOMES AND THE RAISING OF CHILDREN

Far and away the most important change needed for our world is a change of the character of our homes. The preponderance of today's homes are sites of disruption, discord, lacking in conscious commitments to the welfare and safety for the children therein, putting forth programming lessons that are archaic, flawed, punitive, negative concepts taught with negative language and often are simply pathological information.

What really is a home? It is not just a dwelling, not just a house or condo or the building that houses a so-called "home". It includes a subset of the hand-me-down lessons passed on from generations of predecessors who simply echoed the lessons of their experience believing it was good enough for them; therefore, it is alright for their own kids. It is a composite of the minds and hearts of the people who set up the "home". It has to do with the values and virtues that they bring to the establishment of a "home". It is what the people themselves stand for, believe in, practice, and use to define the entity that they call their "home". It doesn't have to be the largest, the newest, and the most elaborate place on the block. It can be whatever the inhabitants want it to be. But ideally, should exude the feelings of love, comfort, safety, congeniality, predictability, modesty and consistency.

Many homes are not built of such qualities but rather are designed to be edifices attesting to the success of the inhabitants, to demonstrate "superiority"; the lavishness that is meant to be a monument to alert observers to the "specialness", of the size, the elaborate construction, the expensive accoutrements that are meant to impress those that have something less.

The home also needs the highest quality of the spirit and thoughts of the inhabitants. A home should reflect the gentleness, the peacefulness, and the kindnesses that take place within. It should echo internally with the patient and loving words that define the people that live there. It should be an oasis for the teaching of love, of patience, of forgiving natures that live and work there. It should be a place where the young can expect to receive consistent support, loving approval, and positive encouragement on a daily basis for what they are learning and adding to their skill sets. It should be devoid of criticism, blame, and anger to control behavior, free of put-downs in the belief that reminding children of their littleness and their lack of competence is a way to stimulate them to better efforts. It should be a home where children are not afraid to bring out their problems for fear of rejection. It should be a place where they can express their frustration about life and not have it ridiculed by the grownups.

It should be a place where the children can expect to learn the right ways to live with each other and to adopt interpersonal working concepts that they can use later in the outside world.

Is all of that too big an expectation of the home of people that brought you into being? Absolutely not. It is a model for every home that intends to raise healthy children for effective lives once they leave the home and take with them the rich and workable lessons that were put forth by devoted parents who taught with uncompromising love.

Anything less is unacceptable as a way of changing our current directions and populating the world with exciting and energized creative new adults.

What would have to change in your present home to match the model mentioned above? What would you have to eliminate from conversations and behavior to assure that fighting and arguments were reduced and preferable not done in the presence of the children? What would you as parents have to give up of your own interests and pursuits to provide time for the children's nurturing? What harsh words, what critical attitudes would have to go to ensure a more peaceful life for your children to remember in later years? How would you plan differently for the activities that would include all family members and be exciting and stimulating for the building of sweet memories for the kids to treasure? How different would that be from your usual way of living that could make such huge differences in the lessons and the remembrances for your kids?

Many parents pride themselves that they get their kids involved in many extraneous activities. One child goes to ballet lessons, another to a swim club, and another to hockey or basketball, or soccer and the parents also believe that appearing at the games is a great sacrifice and gift to their kids. But in the stands listen to the crude and critical remarks that emanate from the parents when their child misses a kick or a basket. Ask them how they think their child feels putting their best effort out only to hear their parents shouting disapproval in front of all the attendees. Is there room for you to change the ways you treat your kids not only in the home but in the outside events as well? Just take a second or two and say to yourself, "How would I feel if someone were yelling invectives toward me at work"? "What if your boss would loudly comment from the water cooler, about some aberration in your office or company plant about your shortfall?

Maybe you are already used to that kind of treatment at work. But you don't have to replicate it for your child in any public forum. Think about the impact of critical and fearful words. Then don't use them!

It only takes a bit of introspection before you utter things, to allow time to make more loving and kinder comments to people. Do it consistently!

There are many people that feel that harshness and hard words in their dealing with the children is necessary to make them work for higher standards. This is a great myth about what kids need. It is detrimental, shaming and humiliating to them and those feelings persist into their adult lives, preventing them from the great performances they are capable of simply because the important people in their childhood didn't know enough to realize that praise and loving correction go a lot farther toward developing healthy challenged and effective performers.

It would be a great contribution to any particular home and even more especially to the transformation of how children in general are raised today. Weigh your priorities for your lives in relationship to your responsibilities to your children. Of course it is important to nourish your workplace and outside relationships but far and away the most important (and the most lacking element of raising children) is the daily lovingly administered interactions we display in the creation of safe and protective environments in our contacts with our precious kids.

CHAPTER 18

WHAT NEEDS TO BE DONE?

In the last chapter on Homes and the Raising of Children, I tried to put a few thoughts together about the kind of home that would be most conducive to the optimal growth of children. You can see that it is not a pie-in-the-sky kind of home. It is simply a home where the primary caregivers are committed to, involved in, consistently active in creating the ambiance that is most favorable for the having and growing of children.

It requires steady and unconditional love, creating an environment in which it is safe at all times for the presence of precious children to live, play, grow, thrive and learn. It would be a home of peace, quietude, absent of anger, fighting, comparing, shaming and humiliating the little inhabitants. Focus would not be on the acquisition of "things" like the latest electronic games, cheap toys, apparatuses that depict space craft or racing cars or other competitive objects vying against each other by the push of thumb buttons with crashes and pursuits and loud noises. For children in need of learning solid lessons about life, love, kindness and togetherness, these toys, games and behaviors are an inane waste of their time that could otherwise be directed toward more appropriate lessons.

In the ideal home, there would be much reduced presence and influence of the TV in the lives of kids. It has been said that by the time a child reaches ten years of age they have already witnessed killing, rape, and mayhem on countless TV programs. We often don't think about it but any stimuli that enter their eyes and access their brains, plant vivid permanent images in their central nervous system. How much better if they hadn't stored maximum violence as part of their mind set.

We didn't used to have such pathological trash for entertainment so how did it come upon us? It was sold by the producers of the programs as what the public wanted to experience and then producers sold the same bill of goods to advertisers. Every night there are a series of FBI, CI and other crime shows that are violent; impressing watchers by competing for the most graphic scenes of crimes and watching depictions of the dregs of our society on the screen. We have the money shows, like Deal or No Deal in which a frenzied audience shout advice to the contestants. We have Super Nanny presenting the worst examples of children who have missed good rearing. We have shows in which the contestants agree to eat all manner of crap to win the monetary prizes.

The point I am getting to relates to the cheapness and gaudiness of our culture today. We are exposed to the bigger-than-we thought process of watching men who have arranged on the Internet to meet teen age decoys presumably for some sex activities. Nothing could more explicitly depict the gross abuses on children than adult men who are so devoid of decency that they stoop to such activity. And, it is amazing that a number of them, when caught, say they knew it was a setup but they went anyway. How desperate and degraded have our people become? The growing decadence of our society has reached epidemic proportions and is rapidly worsening. I put it to you; it has to change and change soon. When most of us seniors were in our childhood such travesties were not even conceived of.

My main reason for this book and the tone of its many chapters is to focus attention on what we have sunk to and what we have to rise out of soon, if we are to preserve the once great society and cultures that America represented to the rest of the world. Our music, our public behaviors, our politicians behavior, our Hollywood contingent, our films, our entertainment and personal interactions are tearing our society apart and there is no evidence on the horizon that many people care about and want to do something about it all.

I am making a plea to those who do have grave concerns that this is not a time to wring our hands in helplessness but rather to talk with one another, to focus attention of others on what is so bad about our life styles and to join forces in working for the necessary changes to, not only stop the current trends but to reestablish honesty, decency, to seek whatever measures necessary to approach the media, the producers of smut and violence to save our precious heritage that we are flaunting so badly at the present.

Having the preponderance of homes disintegrating so drastically, it is no wonder that children born to those homes are subjected to great amounts of negative P-B-A-R experiences, many forms of abuse, punitive measures to keep them manageable, and at the same time indoctrinating them with fear, hate for their perpetrators, frustration with the unfairness of what they have lived through and unpreparedness for the challenges they will face in the harsh outside world.

What would it take to change the scene completely to what we talked about that is necessary for the optimal home? It isn't impossible to entertain such transformation but it will take years of deliberately putting the home, the marriage and the children of that home at the focal point of importance and eliminating all of the negative aspects of living in that home.

How does that happen? It can only occur by the committed, and consistent choices that the parents of any home make to design it to be such a loving, peaceful, safe and healthy home. It is only about making choices for positive attitudes, for loving actions toward all members of that family, for teaching loving interdependency, patience, forgiveness and the determination to have it no other way.

I would urge each of you to do a recapitulation on your own early life. Search out the experiences you were immersed in. What was it like when things went badly because of some bad choices of your parents? What do you recall was positive, consistent, loving and safe that your parents designed into your home?

Again, I insist that you see how central our choices are to the quality of what we will provide for the home. It isn't about more money, more things, more gadgets, and more luxuries. It is about choosing to introduce the true values, the positive things, the loving things, the lasting things that become memories of a rich, happy home life that grows the souls, the minds and the spirits of the members of that family. Then what the children get in terms of loving acceptance, of patience with their learning, with the experience of warm lovingness will be taken eventually to their own homes. When enough people make choices different than they are now making, we will see the quality of family life and the homes change to be rich experiences that will begin to turn our country back to what it is capable of being for an example to the world.

CHAPTER 19

TODAY'S SCENE

This book was my attempt to put down in print what I think happens, starting in the life of a newborn and how the unfolding months and years of early life are so drastically fraught with bad lessons, indescribable modeling by parents, ill-conceived rules for the family of the house, misconceptions, untruths and antiquated practices to impose on children to keep them controlled, quiet and out of the way of the adults who have abdicated their role as monitors of what is going on to allow the present disintegration of the quality of life.

I believe that very few parents are really aware of the intense damage that can be done to the small, growing, learning mind of a child and how their efforts to indoctrinate them into the societal culture are really thinly veiled efforts to make the newcomers "fit" into the paradigms of which ever culture they become a part of in these inane life styles and practices we call modern society. It matters little whether we are talking about life in America with its patterns or in Europe, the Middle East, the Orient or in Africa, each group of constituents of a given race or culture feel that the prime purpose in training children is to perpetuate the customs, the fears, the habits, the acceptable behaviors that fit what the parents grew up in and they wish to maintain.

This has been going on throughout the centuries, and for those same centuries one can see that life was stymied when it was committed to a set of beliefs and behaviors through generational lines. When it is consistently passed down from generation to generation, there is no likely chance that any major changes will occur, even if there is evidence that change is not only necessary but desired by the inhabitants. No one usually has the courage to break step with what is seen as "the way it is" and to suggest a set of new ways of living and doing things.

So many of the practices of our life today can be traced back to the beliefs, the superstitions and fears of our ancestors back through decades. Many of you perhaps have tried to initiate changes, simple different behaviors in your own family culture and have been chastised for trying to break the molds that define society. The pressure from your trainers is usually enough to stop your forward motion toward anything different than they have done for years. In my dealing with families over the years in my medical practice, I can recall many instances when elderly 70-90 year-olds still insist that the family toe the mark on issues that have long ago become not only outmoded but many that are downright counterproductive to the rearing of healthy, creative, energized children. Life has outgrown such ideas but the seniors don't want to acknowledge the need for things to be upgraded or even discarded when they are no longer effective in fostering children who can think for themselves when they reach adulthood.

I am reminded of a passage in a book by Neal Donald Walsch in which he presents a set of steps that could and should impact our limited thinking on many issues. In the case of this book it is referring to the need to reexamine the core beliefs we have promoted through the ages about life and our spirituality. I would urge everyone to get and read this important book, **_"The New Revelations"_** by Walsch.

"Five Things You Can Choose Now"

1. *You can choose to acknowledge that some of your old beliefs about God and Life are no longer working.*

2. *You can choose to acknowledge that there is something you do not understand about God and Life, the understanding of which will change every thing.*

3. *You can choose to be willing for a new understanding of God and Life to now be brought forth, an understanding that could produce a new way of life on your planet.*

4. *You can choose to be courageous enough to explore and examine this new understanding and, if it aligns with your inner truth and knowing, to enlarge your beliefs system to include it.*

5. *You can choose to live your lives as demonstrations of your highest and grandest beliefs, rather than as denials of them.*

This is a set of five invitations to simply rethink the concepts you have been given and acquired during your life up to now and to consider that rethinking and restructuring your belief system is overdue.

To his point #1, no one could really believe that we have trucked down the highway of life with a set of archaic beliefs about God and Life that is outdated and not worthy of continuing to set the standards for our beliefs and behavior. We are a "modern culture" that has lost all semblance of decency in every aspect of our daily living, which espouses and practices the worst kinds of business practices as evidenced by Enron, Tycos and countless other companies that operate on paradigms that are pathological, that perpetuate the myth that the people at the top of our corporations are all wise, all creative, are to be trusted with the assets of huge companies, and are not to be questioned in their shoddy adherence to the power and control tactics that they impose on their employees. If you doubt the truth of my words, please take the time to read **_"The Paradigm Conspiracy"_** by Breton and Largent for a true picture of the corporate world of America. Or read the book, **_"Good to Great"_** by Jim Collins, to learn what the well run companies do that is lacking in thousands of other businesses. It is a truth that I hate to admit but the America that was so great and so effective at the helm of good things happening, is no longer the sterling model for the rest of the world to emulate. We are on the slippery slope to second-class status because of how we have not perpetuated the principles and standards that got us there in the first place.

Taking the #1 concept of Walsch above and paraphrase the sentence to read, _we can choose to acknowledge that there is something about common decency, about relationships with one another, about fair play, about the misuse of anger and violence to control others, about the absence of love in our relationships, and about our interpersonal practices that are no longer working._

Every necessary structure of modern life has been ignored and corroded in the past decades when our interests and attention have been preoccupied with comfort, ease, letting important issues go, to the detriment of our very life on this planet.

Public education is a shame and a fraud and a miserable failure in taking the young minds of our children through an exciting exploration of what is possible. What could learning really be like for children if the broken-down systems could be restored to an effective mode of learning devoid of the teacher's union that hobbles the advent of any effective change and that teachers were required to prove mandatory ongoing training to improve their skills.

I am appalled when I consider that the educational courses for future teachers are so flimsy as to produce individuals incapable of handling the chore of providing exciting, energizing learning for our children. I think it is a blatant crime that in this country of such great resources that we are still operating on the model for public education that was conceived by and promoted by the early industrial geniuses that said all they wanted the people to learn in school was "reading, writing and arithmetic" so they could perform the basic tasks that industrial labor needed to master for shop performance.

A child graduating from high school today (with their head full of crazy concepts about life derived from their trip through the family experience of programming and control) decides to enter college and become a teacher. The curricular segments of becoming an educator are unchanged for all practical purposes over the last decades. Here again any nuances to enhance the content of educational training are also discouraged by the union which is hell bent on keeping things "the same and controllable." After four years of college the graduates are dumped on the scene to look for teaching jobs that they are ill prepared for. Further, the standards for behavior in the classrooms have sunk so low that the students that are disinterested in learning, so disrupt the class that the other students don't have a fair chance for full concentration on the subjects at hand.

My wife and I had a period of being partners in the Visioneering Group whose intent was to take new learning into both the corporate and the educational world. We were using new concepts about how to think as embodied in the work of Ned Herrmann and we taught the newest information on how we really use our brains. The lessons said that there was a difference between the way the two sides of our brains approach living and learning. It is genius information and has over the past several decades found its deserved attention in corporate as well as educational America.

The information contends that the left and right side of the brain are very different in the way each handles coming information; the left side is very structured, precise, detailed and applies best to topics like math, logic, finance, and bottom-line issues. It also explains the left brain's aptitude in planning, controlling, maintaining established and proven practices.

The right side of our brain is less structured, less interested in control and sameness and deals with the things that affect our personal relationships, it is the creative side of all brains, it is "more playful", more adventurous, more fun than the left side and it sees the forest rather than the detail of each individual tree that makes the forest.

This information that Ned Herrmann has given to the world explains why some people are born to be more left or right and why their strengths and attributes depend on the dominant hemisphere of their brain.

One startling conclusion that my wife and I came to was to realize that there are left and right thinking children in every classroom. This was news to many teachers. There was an awareness that kids do think differently but when it is put in the context of seeing the differences as resulting from the genetic predisposition to be either left or right brain from the start of life, it lends itself to better understand that the so-called ADD and ADHD are characteristics of right brained children trying to adjust to a basically left brained educational system. Rather than being a structural flaw in the child, it is more the confusion of seeing the world from the right brain rather than the left side. It was designed that way to enhance the varieties of thinking that are possible by appreciating that each side has a major contribution to make rather than being seen as a major flaw to be suppressed and dealt with.

Unfortunately for many thousands of children they were identified as have a "sickness" and given the label of ADD and put on Ritalin to control their characteristics that disturb the classroom and present the teacher with having to "control" these right-brained inquisitive and eager-to-learn bright children to maintain order and decorum in the classroom. Left brained kids accept information without protest, the things that match their Brainedness. The right-sided thinkers are more prone to question established concepts and ideas. In doing so they appear to be disruptive and a nuisance rather than capable of contributing a new perspective to be considered. Right-brained kids are unusually bright, they get the classroom lessons quickly and get bored by repetition that the left-brainer need. It is this boredom and the impatience of children who have already grasped the concepts that contribute to the restlessness of the right-brained kids and contribute to their "reputation" as troublemakers who need to be quelled by medications. Instead of medicating them to quiet them down, change the curricular segments of the school to be more challenging and relevant to today's world.

During the days of working with the classes and the teachers, it was also a revelation to find that many of the teachers had miserable penmanship and on many occasions they were also faulty in spelling ordinary words of the language. If they don't know where they are flawed as teachers, how are they in a position to teach meaningfully? Just take a minute or two and think back to the variety of teachers you had contact with in school and college years. Which ones did you learn the most from and which blur in your memory as being less effective.

Change directions of your thinking for a moment. There is a rapidly growing belief that many of the difficulties that have befallen our lives have been generated by our churches that have failed to keep up with the viable leadership in the area of our spiritual needs. The God of yesterday, presented as a punitive, wrathful God who was always looking for our transgressions so we could receive proper chastisement no longer fits in a world that is in need of the unconditional love mentioned in spiritual writings. We need a new way to do church so it can be not just a Sunday hour listening to drab and irrelevant stale thoughts about the "old Sunday school God." Going back to Walsh's comment we need to acknowledge that our old ideas about God and Life are not longer working for us. It is necessary that the spiritual portion of our daily lives be enlarged to the state where it is with us in all we do, and not just isolated to an occasional symbolic ritual when we think of it.

We need leadership to help us see that most of what we do today in relationship to one another is predicated on seeing how separate from one another we consider ourselves to be. In newer thought there is really no separation between us at all. We are all children of one God and that makes us siblings to one another. Let's consider acting as though we are similar human beings trying to make sense out of life as we see it around us. The violence, the anger, the character assassination, the withholding of love and cooperation from one another, the cheating, the deceit, the gossip and segregation have and continue to create a climate of mini-warfare in our everyday lives and we end up seeing one another as adversaries or even enemies that deserve our attacks.

It is late, very late in our evolution to be recognizing the issues that are destroying ourselves and the planet on which we live. I do not believe it is inevitable that we can do nothing to change things toward a new world. But what we now continue to do daily is only taking us farther down the slope.

It's an old story but we need to get ourselves into concern for one another, we need to embrace the concept of unconditional love toward one another, we need to realize that the most important job we have is to change the way we raise children. When you stop and think about a design for raising healthy, un–abused, children it is evident that each child born to a set of parents is a 2 decade responsibility for each child if we want to assure a new and healthy young adult population that can assume the tasks and responsibilities of effective living, working and relating.

It means putting the welfare and learning of the child ahead of our adult interests, not relying on TV as a surrogate baby-sitter, not depending on day care to handle the early lessons for our children, not allowing the same ones that screwed up our own early life lessons to determine what is best for the child. Grandparents are often quite opinionated about proper nurturing methods) the same ones they used on you). and they are ever present to tell you what is wrong about our variances from their thinking. It is time for new paradigms to become active in the raising of children. Disregard the efforts by grandparents to insist that they "know better".

At present, the state of our young adults, preoccupied with self-indulgence, rocked with anger about what they experienced in their early years, and having missed the serious elements of essential education and self-discipline raises the question about what we can expect when they really take over the leading of our country into the future. We are already taking on the characteristics of a second or third rate power in the world today. Our children, in their schools, are behind children in other countries who will be their competitors in the future for a world position. Unchecked, it can only go further and faster down the slope to historical oblivion unless radical changes are made and made now by coalescing our mutual concerns into an effective organ for remedial alterations.

This is not simply the musings of a disgruntled guy who has lived in the best of what we had and is now realizing what we are losing. It is my plea to everyone to give up the shallow life styles that

118

you engage in, to get serious about the task at hand in reversing our cataclysmic failures at creating and sustaining the paradise that is possible when we give up current practices that are pushing us over the brink.

If you don't have enough yet to concern you about the state of affairs in America, consider the unbelievable performances in our Houses of Congress, the individual characteristics of our so-called statesmen, the lack of constructive legislating that comes from our alcoholic, alternative life-styled and incompetent representatives that are shaping the directions and character of our country. That should be enough to scare the hell out of you. But try to get something done about it. Many of the worst of our politicians have been in their positions for decades of their incompetence, protected from being un-elected because they have become so adept at using "pork" and other prizes for leaving them in place. This country was not designed and built by the likes of what we see every day in the news. And speaking about "news", we are daily inundated by warped journalism, the news media molding the stories out of context to be supportive of the "sick" political machinations in our capital cities.

Never before have we so badly needed monumental change in the practices and the people who are steering our public and national lives in wrong directions. It is the recipe for the downfall of all that has been right about America and there are precious few individuals that are sounding the clarion call for change.

This book represents my own ideas about the whole subject of what we are deeply enmeshed in watching the deterioration of what has been the grandest and most effective culture the world has ever seen. It was founded by courageous and determined individuals who were escaping from the breakdown of the quality of life in England and continental Europe. There were terrific sacrifices by them in daring to launch out and construct a new country with hopes, dreams and ambitions that surpassed anything ever seen prior to its emergence. Like all other cultures, empires and civilizations it had meager beginnings that gradually grew, stood the test of time and provided human living conditions never before seen on Earth. We have had troubles, wars, internal struggles, difficulty in main-lining the development of our Republic but America weathered the many challenges.

Somewhere along the line we began to believe in our own superiority and elegance based on success that came to us but inevitably our confidence in ourselves and our country have become taken for granted, we have lost touch with the need to constantly upgrade, protect and expand the foundational truths.

Today, there are many evidences of our demise across the board. Greed, selfishness, envy of one another, hoarding for our own purposes and allowing indifference and living lives that took direction from such books as *"Looking Out for Number One"* and countless other books of similar ilk that foster the idea of aggrandizement of self at any cost to those with whom we share the planet.

We can witness the tawdriness of our current state by looking at the various systems that were originally constructed for progress and then look at the erosion of our commercial status, the corporate failures engineered by self-seeking CEO's and leaders hell bent in getting all they can regardless of who else suffers.

Look at our educational record with our kids falling farther and farther behind many of the third-world kids in acquiring necessary education.

Look at the corrupt political scene at all levels of government and the pathological people who hold lofty positions for self gain and to reassure reelection. Both Houses of Congress are loaded with members unworthy of holding their positions and still the populace that is also in a slump continues to send them back to Washington.

Health care is not exempt from these considerations. We have the greatest technology and achievements in delivering high grade care, but the medical system is still fighting tooth and nail for taking more out of the system than in inventing new ways to use our resources economically and effectively.

Nor are our churches free of involvement. The Catholic church with its involvement in pedophilia over perhaps centuries is a disgrace and other churches are being led by clergy who don't have a grasp of what is going on.

Marriage, unwed pregnancies, child abuse, mounting rates of divorce and fractured homes that contribute to the whole text of this book continue unabatedly to defile the very institutions of family, marriage, homes, providing safety and guidance for the young in their journey to adulthood.

I am hoping that readers will begin to clearly see what is still reversible but it is perhaps the toughest battle we are confronted with and we need to address it as a life / death issue for our nation and society. Please don't take the easy way out. It leads to perdition and mayhem. My fondest blessings go out to all of you. It is a do-able challenge that we can meet but we must give our full attention to the process.

Thank you for being concerned.

APPENDIX

PROGRAMMING   **BELIEFS**   **ACTIONS**   **RESULTS**

RULES
SHOULDS
SHOULDN'TS
RIGHT / WRONG
GOOD / BAD
SMART / DUMB
ALWAYS....
NEVER...
CAN / CAN'T
MUST DO
"MY WAY"
WILL WORK
WON'T WORK
"THE WAY IT IS"

This is how your life training begins as an infant. Your young parents, having limited experience in raising kids, <u>can only give you</u> what they "<u>know</u>" about the process, and that often is no more than what was done to them when they were little. What they know has its limits, is not necessarily true, might even be wrong or distorted but those are the only lessons they can give from their parenting skills. And you are under pressure to learn it their way and fit into the mold that has family and societal sanction.

P ➡ B ➡ A ➡ R

PROGRAMMING   BELIEFS   ACTIONS   RESULTS

PROGRAMMING	BELIEFS
RULES	**BELIEFS**
SHOULDS	**EXPECTATIONS**
SHOULDN'TS	**ASSUMPTIONS**
RIGHT / WRONG	**HABITS**
GOOD / BAD	**PREJUDICE**
SMART / DUMB	**"FILTERS"**
ALWAYS....	**PARADIGMS**
NEVER...	**EGO**
CAN / CAN'T	**"TRUTH"**
MUST	
"MY WAY"	
WILL WORK	
WON'T WORK	
"WAY IT IS"	

With repetition, reinforcement and insistence on the learning of the programming, those rules and parameters for our behavior are assimilated into the subconscious of the child as the "truth" and become the "catalog of beliefs" the child is expected to live by.

As we can all recall from our own early days, there will be repercussions for failing to follow the "party line". This set of learned (and automatic responses) then becomes the "autopilot" that will determine our course of behavior hence forth.

P ➡ **B** ➡ **A** ➡ **R**

PROGRAMMING   **BELIEFS**   **ACTIONS**   **RESULTS**

RULES	BELIEFS	WHAT YOU DO
SHOULDS	EXPECTATIONS	DECISIONS
SHOULDN'TS	ASSUMPTIONS	CHOICES
RIGHT / WRONG	HABITS	OMISSIONS
GOOD / BAD	PREJUDICE	
SMART / DUMB	"FILTERS"	
ALWAYS....	PARADIGMS	
NEVER...	EGO	
CAN / CAN'T	"TRUTH"	
MUST DO		
"MY WAY"		
WILL WORK		
WON'T WORK	Slide 2	
"WAY IT IS"		

Once the beliefs, and assumptions about life and the
world are firmly established, that belief system becomes the driving
force for how we will behave. Our actions, and decisions will be
consistent with and in accord with the beliefs we learned so well and
hold as our behavioral guidelines. Begin to see that the beliefs
developed from the earlier programming give rigid definition to how
we conduct our lives. Unless the beliefs are altered, the style of what
we do will remain consistent (and limited to) what we hold to be "true".

P ➤ B ➤ A ➤ R

PROGRAMMING	BELIEFS	ACTIONS	RESULTS
RULES	BELIEFS	WHAT YOU DO	**OUTCOMES**
SHOULDS	EXPECTATIONS	DECISIONS	**RESULTS**
SHOULDN'TS	ASSUMPTIONS	CHOICES	**WHAT YOU GET**
RIGHT / WRONG	HABITS	OMISSIONS	**YOUR REALITY**
GOOD / BAD	PREJUDICE		
SMART / DUMB	"FILTERS"		
ALWAYS....	PARADIGMS		
NEVER...	EGO		
CAN / CAN'T	"TRUTH"		
MUST			
MY WAY			
WILL WORK			
WON'T WORK			
DON'T YOU			
DARE			

Because our programming established our belief system and our beliefs determine how we will act and behave, the results of our efforts in life will always be consistent with the quality and limits of actions stemming from what we believe is possible (for us).

Try as we might, to change the outcomes by trying harder to do what we believe, it is still true...

"If you always do what you've always done...
You'll always get what you have always gotten."

P-BAR REVISITED

P ➡ B ➡ A ➡ R

PROGRAMMING   BELIEFS   ACTIONS   RESULTS

RULES   BELIEFS   WHAT YOU DO   OUTCOMES
SHOULDS   EXPECTATIONS DECISIONS   RESULTS
SHOULDN'TS   ASSUMPTIONS   CHOICES   WHAT YOU GET
RIGHT / WRONG HABITS   OMISSIONS   YOUR REALITY
GOOD / BAD   PREJUDICE
SMART / DUMB   "FILTERS"
ALWAYS....   PARADIGMS
NEVER...   EGO
CAN / CAN'T   "TRUTH"
MUST
MY WAY
WILL WORK
WON'T WORK
DON'T YOU
DARE

➡

Your journey from infancy to adulthood was directed and controlled by parents and society. That makes you a pawn of their design. They couldn't have done it differently but you can now choose to change your current reality by reversing the PBAR formula as follows.

128

P ← B ← A ← R

PROGRAMMING	BELIEFS	ACTIONS	RESULTS
RULES	BELIEFS	WHAT YOU DO	OUTCOMES
SHOULDS	EXPECTATIONS	DECISIONS	RESULTS
SHOULDN'TS	ASSUMPTIONS	CHOICES	WHAT YOU GET
RIGHT / WRONG	HABITS	OMISSIONS	"YOUR REALITY"
GOOD / BAD	PREJUDICE		
SMART / DUMB	"FILTERS"		
ALWAYS....	PARADIGMS		
NEVER...	EGO		
CAN / CAN'T	"TRUTH"		
MUST			
MY WAY			
WILL WORK			
WON'T WORK			
DON'T YOU			
DARE			

You are now going to design your very own plan to produce a life that will take you to new heights and toward a new set of goals –this time of your own choosing.

So look at the "R" of your current life and what results you are not pleased with. You can now ask yourself a question that will start a new life for you.

Ask. *"What would I like different than what I am currently experiencing?"* This is the time of choosing new outcomes, new goals and a different realty than you currently have. *"What would my life look like if it was the way I want it to be?"*

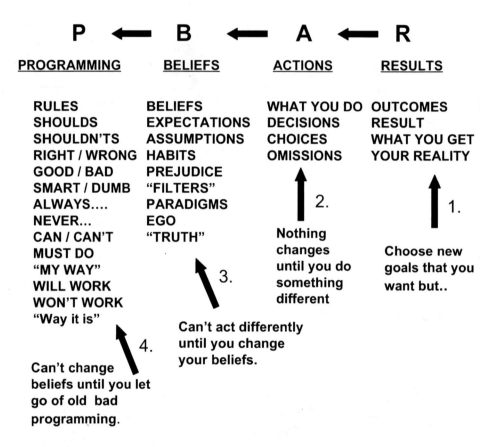

PROGRAMMING	BELIEFS	ACTIONS	RESULTS
RULES	BELIEFS	WHAT YOU DO	OUTCOMES
SHOULDS	EXPECTATIONS	DECISIONS	RESULT
SHOULDN'TS	ASSUMPTIONS	CHOICES	WHAT YOU GET
RIGHT / WRONG	HABITS	OMISSIONS	YOUR REALITY
GOOD / BAD	PREJUDICE		
SMART / DUMB	"FILTERS"		
ALWAYS....	PARADIGMS		
NEVER...	EGO		
CAN / CAN'T	"TRUTH"		
MUST DO			
"MY WAY"			
WILL WORK			
WON'T WORK			
"Way it is"			

2. Nothing changes until you do something different

1. Choose new goals that you want but..

3. Can't act differently until you change your beliefs.

4. Can't change beliefs until you let go of old bad programming.

At first this may sound difficult but...All it requires is for you to spend time revisiting the early days when inexperienced and unknowing parents grasped at ideas about raising you. All the programming was only someone's thoughts and not sacrosanct ways of developing effective people. Instead, the programming was hodge-podge and should be removed from your unconscious and make room for a serious upgrade about how you want your life to go.

130

ISBN 1553690020-6

9 781553 690207